April 3, 2015

To Arden,

    Let the Business
Reformation Begin!

[signature]

Endorsements

Chief Leadership Officer is rich in content and inventive in delivery. The narrative form makes the wisdom and knowledge Kevin has experienced over five decades in business accessible to anyone interested in leadership and innovative business principles. *Chief Leadership Officer* is an extraordinary road map for leading a life and organization with a concise purpose and clear values.

Dr. Nido Qubein
President, High Point University

Kevin W. McCarthy has long been on the cutting edge of what works in leadership. His latest contribution, *Chief Leadership Officer*, provides a road map for those executives who recognize that what has worked well in the past will not effectively meet the challenges of the future. Read it and adapt accordingly.

George Morrisey
Author of nineteen books including *Management By Objectives and Results* and the three-book series *Morrisey on Planning*

As the role of the CEO has evolved from improving financial performance and exceeding shareholder expectations to being a CLO, this book takes us on an enlightened journey of discovery where the true wealth of a company—its people—can be increased to achieve individual and team performance on an unparalleled scope. *Chief Leadership Officer* is a hands-on blueprint for CEOs to smoothly transition to become their company's CLO, on-purpose leaders in this, the Digital Age and beyond.

Gordie Allen
Sales Prospecting Trainer, Leads-Plus, Inc.

Chief Leadership Officer just blew me away! As the President of the Central Florida Christian Chamber of Commerce, I saw myself as being an "incompletely right" CLO. I'm ready to be in the CLO Foundry.

Mark Goldstein
President, Central Florida Christian Chamber of Commerce

Kevin W. McCarthy brilliantly demystifies real leadership within our digital, 24/7, diverse and inherently complicated world. Through a captivating and exciting business parable, *Chief Leadership Officer* is more than a "cutesy corporate fashion statement" but a fresh, dynamic, and amazingly doable process for leaders to powerfully align their company's three bottom-lines: Profit, People and Purpose. If you desire to increase purposeful wealth for yourself, your team, and your communities, I exhort you to become a CLO.

Dr. Jim Harris
Advisor to leaders, executive coach, and author of 14 award-winning business books

Over three decades of being in business I've traveled from entrepreneur to CEO. I immediately recognized and embraced the benefits and value of becoming a CLO. The CLO way of doing business is more real and relevant to the realities of the current (and coming) business environment. Legally, I'm still a CEO. In my leadership and operation, I'm all CLO.

Tana Greene
CEO-CLO
Blue Bloodhound, Inc.

Bestselling Author of *The On-Purpose Business Person*
and *The On-Purpose Person*

Kevin W. McCarthy

Chief
LEADERSHIP
~~Executive~~
Officer

INCREASING WEALTH
SO EVERYONE PROFITS

Notices

Chief Leadership Officer is a story with fictional characters. Generally, any resemblance to actual persons, living or dead, is entirely coincidental.

The methods and models espoused in this book are based on the personal and professional experiences of the author working with a compilation of collaborators and clients over decades. Some of the anecdotal illustrations and stories are based on composites and embellishments of actual situations but remain fictionalized.

ON PURPOSE®
publishing

PO Box 1568, Winter Park, FL 32790-1568

www.on-purpose.com

Dedication
Judith Haskell McCarthy

In the fall of 1980, Judith and I met as Section A classmates at The Darden School, the graduate business school on the grounds of The University of Virginia.

Judith is a "poet" (the b-school term for liberal arts undergraduate majors) who was making a career change from working in higher education. I, on the other hand, was upgrading my entrepreneurial inclination and aptitude to gain better business skills, thinking, language, and methods.

As friends and poor full-time graduate students, our dutch treat dinners often included sharing carrot cake: one cut, one chose. In those dinner conversations, she fretted over who would hire her. I fretted I would get hired and my entrepreneurial spirit would be crushed. Upon our graduation in May of 1982, Judith worked in Hartford, CT. I was hired to work in Orlando, FL. By August of 1983, I launched a start-up while she remained gainfully employed.

On April 7, 1984, we completed our M&A and married. Judith says, "I willingly transferred my flag onto your ship" and has unwaveringly abided in her decision. In time, we had two spin-offs: Charles and Anne.

Today, she still frets mostly over our family and me! And I still venture. We've made it work. Actually, I've made it work for her—hard work!

Judith, your North Augusta, SC, friends were right, I am so-o lucky I married you. (There's a funny story behind that; ask me when we meet.)

Thank you Judith for "willingly transferring your flag" and trusting me most through the rough seas of life and for being an anchor through it all. That's true dedication!

Love ya!
Kevin

CEO-to-CLO™

"Something has to change!" How many times have you heard this said in an organization?

Actually, some*one*, not some*thing*, has to change. CEOs are infrequently challenged directly. Yet, I've made a living out of speaking to CEOs with candor. This book is no exception. Contrary to popular notions, CEOs are rarely arrogant. Most are smart, hungry learners who are eager for insights and improvements to their leadership and business.

The premise of this book's message and movement is simple. The title and role of a CEO is obsolete. The role is a command and control holdout mired in the archaic thinking and ways of the Industrial Age. We're well into the Digital Age and into the Age of Purpose and Meaning.

New times call for new leadership. The emerging business leaders will be called Chief Leadership Officers (CLOs). They carry three straightforward charges:

1. Position the organization to be a leader in its chosen field.
2. Position each person to be leaders on and off their jobs.
3. Meaningfully integrate the two above to be increasing wealth so everyone profits—remembering that financial gain is but one aspect of profit.

CLOs authentically embrace the business of business and people, not as "human resources," but as human beings—the crucial contributors to organizational innovation and success.

For the typical business person much of what lives in this story will appear familiar. On the other hand, many of the CLO constructs, models, and terms will, at a minimum, disturb your thinking and give you pause to reflect on your leadership competency. Hopefully, you'll find yourself saying, "Wow, there really is a better way of leading in business."

Let the Business Reformation Begin!
Kevin W. McCarthy

CONTENTS

Read This First!

You have a role in this story. Over the pages of *Chief Leadership Officer* you enter into two conversations. The first conversation takes place in the present with Chris, your sharp-witted business colleague, and his longtime friend known to us only as the Chief Leadership Officer or CLO.

Within this conversation the CLO recounts his formative journey of becoming a Chief Leadership Officer. He shares lessons learned as guided by Pops, his great-grandfather, and Bob Scott, the CLO of a large international company.

Icons are provided to distinguish one conversation from the other. The icon for the present conversation is three steaming coffee mugs (below), symbolic of Chris, the CLO, and you sharing mugs of coffee at a fictional cafe called Latte Out Loud. (Fun tip: find the chapter with a special variation of this icon.) The book starts in the present.

The CLO logo (below) indicates dialogue when the CLO is recounting his CEO-to-CLO awakening and transition.

CLO

With the exceptions of the Prologue, Chapter 1, and the Epilogue, each chapter opens with the CLO's reminiscing his development. In the other chapters his reflection is followed by the banter of Chris and the CLO. Your job is to be with them soaking in the conversation while pondering the notion and precepts of being a Chief Leadership Officer. Enjoy!

Prologue
You Run Things

You run things. You make decisions. You manage a P&L. People look to you for direction and answers. You want very satisfied customers. You willingly weigh the risks and the rewards in order to make sound decisions that move the business forward.

You know the feelings of being overwhelmed and low as well as the joys and the highs of success. You persistently pursue improvement. You seek more—a better life, family, team, and customers. You strive to make a difference and make money. You willingly grasp the reigns of the beast called a business because its possibilities are endless.

Amid your inspiration, aspiration, and perspiration lives frustration. Yes, you're a Chief Executive Officer, even if not in official title, because in reality we're all running something.

Chapter 1
Hey, It's Just a Cup of Coffee

The task of an executive is not to change human beings.
Rather as the Bible tells us in the parable of the talents, the
task is to multiply the performance capacity of the whole
by putting to use whatever strength,
whatever health, whatever aspiration there is in individuals.

Peter F. Drucker
The Effective Executive
Management Consultant, Educator, and Author
1909–2005

Your smartphone rings and up pops the name and image
of Chris, a wisecracking good friend and respected CEO
colleague. You smile. One can never tell what this spirited guy
is up to, but he's typically fun and interesting.

"Hi, Chris."

"Drop everything! Join me. Come grab a cup of coffee
with an old friend of mine who's in town for just a couple
more hours. He invited me to attend some presentation he did
earlier this morning. I was already booked but free in the
afternoon. I'm just about to pick him up and then take him to
the airport. We're stopping for a jolt of java at Latte Out
Loud, a coffee shop someone at his conference recommended
to him. You two will enjoy getting to know one another. You
in?"

Scanning your calendar quickly you see it is free. "Yeah,
see you there. I've never been there, but I know the place. It's
one of those funky independent coffeehouses near the airport."

Chris says, "Great! I'll have a mug of coffee waiting for

you. Black, right? Hurry over. This should be interesting!"
You detect a hint of sarcasm in his voice.

What's Chris up to?

Intrigued about your impromptu meeting and Chris's
mystery friend, you arrive and park your car in an open spot
at the front door of the cafe. Getting a good parking spot is
always great. Fresh coffee aroma and two baristas greet you.

As promised, there's a steamy ceramic coffee mug awaiting
you. Introductions are made. You sit down. The conversation
begins.

The Intervention

Chris and his friend clearly have a good history, albeit
with Chris it is bound to be a bit offbeat. He's the kind of guy
who drives an expensive car, wears fancy watches, and carries
a wad of hundred dollars bills just because "I like the feel of
cash in my hands." For all his color and show, he's a good
friend, devoted family man, and astute businessman.

You pick up on the familiarity of this warm and well-
worn friendship going back to days on the playground. Chris
and you have a great relationship begun in your respective
adult working years. You're honored that Chris invited you to
be a part of his reunion.

Given that his friend has a flight to catch, Chris seems
unusually anxious to move the conversation along. Cutting
short the small talk, he suggests a business card exchange. You
each oblige him.

Chris grabs his friend's business card out of your hand only
to flash it right in front of your eyes. He points his fingertip to
the job title. With a cackle, Chris demands of you, "Read this.
Out loud."

Unsure of Chris's motivation, you comply and read it
aloud, "Chief Leadership Officer."

Chris turns to his friend and with a syrupy drip of teasing
says, "Well Mr. Chief Leadership Officer, before I put you on

the plane back home to Pittsburgh, tell us the story of why you call yourself *that* instead of a Chief Executive Officer. Did you get a CEO demotion or something? Start from the top."

Chris turns to you and mocks, "I've been waiting to hear this for some time! I mean really, a Chief Leadership Officer. How fashionable!"

Turning to his friend, Chris chides him further, "Really? Why don't you just call yourself a CEO like the rest of us? No. You've got to be special. Got to be different. A 'CLO.' What gives?"

Taking the ribbing in stride, Chris's friend says, "If I didn't know you cared so much I'd think you didn't care at all. Most of all I'm happy you finally learned to read."

You think, *Touché, Mr. CLO. This should be fun!*

The CLO and you exchange looks in mutual realization that this is more than a cup of coffee. It's an intervention!

Admittedly, you're curious. You think, *A Chief Leadership Officer? What is that anyway? A fancy title for the head of HR? Is that like the lead trainer or something else?*

Rather than coddle Chris's antics, the Chief Leadership Officer offers a direct response, "A few years ago I transitioned from being a CEO to a CLO. I'm still the top officer in my company."

"Why?" asks Chris.

"In a nutshell, a CLO is a more complete leadership approach than a CEO. A CLO has a heart for service, a head for profit, the resilience of the military, and a moral imperative. Our value of 'Everyone Profits' calls for high mastery of management and leadership to integrate and produce an abundance of positive results. We all exist to increase the wealth of the world. I'll explain it more if you wish."

"So-o-o noble," teases Chris. "You said 'we.' There's more like you? Can't a CEO do the same thing and keep the title?"

"No. Words carry meaning and emphasis. A Chief

Executive Officer's job is to execute or carry out plans. A Chief *Leadership* Officer's job is to lead. Changing my title is a clean break from the CEO-run system and patterns of the past. Being a CLO better represents my true role and responsibilities to my stakeholders."

"Hmmm," lets out Chris. "Interesting, as in blind date interesting," alluding to the quip that a person described as "interesting" is code for ugly and strange.

Chris challenges, "What's different from being a CEO?"

"A CLO has three major charges. The first is to position the organization be a leader in its chosen field.

"The second is to position the people to be leaders on and off their jobs.

"The third is to integrate the prior two to be increasing wealth so everyone profits—a caveat being that financial gain is but one aspect of wealth and profit."

As this extemporaneous inquisition begins, you sense a mix of personal amusement and curiosity to learn more. Chris, the former trial attorney turned real estate developer success story, cross-examines his long-time friend. *This should be fascinating. Hey, it's just a cup of coffee.*

The Chief Leadership Officer is graciously good-humored with Chris and unfazed by Chris's boisterous manner. In fact, he seems accustomed to and entertained by Chris's antics.

Chris opens his "deposition" of the CLO with, "Let's start with the backstory. How did this fanciful CLO thing start?"

"Chris, you probably remember my Pops, my great-grandfather." And so the CLO mounts his "defense."

Chapter 2
The Chief Leadership Officer

You take the blue pill, the story ends.
You wake up in your bed
and believe whatever you want to believe.
You take the red pill, you stay in Wonderland,
and I show you how deep the rabbit hole goes.

Morpheus speaking to Neo
The Matrix, 1999

CLO

My epiphany happened at my Pops' 100th birthday party in his assisted living facility. Our family had just sung "Happy Birthday," and we were eating cake. Pops was seated. I leaned down to give him a hug. As I pulled away, he grasped my shoulders with his bony hands, looked me in the eyes and asked me a simple, typically rather ordinary, question, "How's business for my Great-Grandchild?"

Pops, a retired business owner, and I often talked business. But, here, on his 100th birthday, I wavered. At a social event like this, do I give a polite response like, "Fine. Everything's fine"? Or, do I answer honestly and say, "I'm miserable"— words I've been unwilling to utter to myself, let alone say to someone else?

Over the recent years, discontentment had been welling up within me. Something was wrong. Wrong with me? Wrong with my business? Wrong with the business world? I couldn't put my finger on it. I had this sense that regardless of whether the revenues got better or even worse, I was somehow going to be worse off. I figured if the business makes more money, then at least I'm winning at something. Plus, I could afford to distract myself from this deep gnawing inside me.

But this was Pops who was asking. I lowered the wall of my defenses. "Pops, my business is making money; but I'm miserable. Something's wrong. I sense it. I'm overwhelmed and overworked. I'm killing myself keeping it all together. I'd like to hire someone to do my job."

Within my family, this confession nearly rose to the level of entrepreneurial heresy. We're a family of business owners going back eleven generations. By all appearances, it seemed that I too carried this highly curated entrepreneurial gene. The creative act of an idea being conceived, birthed, and raised into a productive and profitable reality called "a business" is oddly irresistible. Talk of business is what I heard growing up around the dinner table and at family gatherings. I genuinely felt called and equipped as a business owner.

My best friend from high school and I were in college together when we started the business. He was a tech whiz and I had the business brains and experience having worked in family businesses since I was a little kid. He did software development and operations while I focused on the marketing, clients, business administration, and finances. In those days our org chart was "filled" with just two names: his and mine.

I grew up working in various family businesses. Pops started and owned a specialty foundry. One summer in high school I worked in it long enough to know it wasn't for me. My Grandfather, Pop's son, had an electronics housing and enclosures plastics molding and fabrication business. I had summer jobs there, too. My father's business designed and manufactured specialty electronic components. Between the three companies, I had worked at one time or another in every department. Opening a business was second nature, or so I thought.

Yet, now I doubted myself, *If I am this prepared for being a CEO, then why am I so weighted with concern and*

A Rising Star

The day of my confession at Pops' birthday party I was the twenty-five-year-old "rising star CEO" of a thriving small business employing over twenty people with revenues in the low seven figures. My cofounder and I hired talented friends from high school and college to help part time. As our client base grew, many of them graduated to full-time employees. Working with friends offered a wonderful blend of social and business interaction. It also carried the strain and blur of personal involvement outside the workplace.

When people asked me what I was doing, I took pride in handing out my business card with the CEO title on it and saying, "I'm the CEO of a tech start-up that helps our clients with online security and data protection."

The honeymoon of a business start-up was giving way to the day-to-day routine of actually running a business. What my position and my employees were requiring—dare I say, demanding—of me, left me feeling unfit and ill-prepared. From our customers' point of view, we had our act together. Behind the scenes, however, we were a dysfunctional mess.

My trajectory as the young CEO was apparently newsworthy. The local business journal carried stories headlining me as "The Local Biz Whiz Kid," and such. The business was long on promise and opportunity but short on satisfaction. The team would read articles about me and scoff at my public persona versus the real me. Instead of encouraging pride in our accomplishments, the articles distanced us from one another in an awkward "us and them" tradition found in management and labor relationships.

Privately, I was barely treading water trying to keep the business and my head above the choppy waters in the seemingly endless flood of responsibilities. Each stage of growth brought with it added levels of business complexity, governmental regulations, and employee problems.

How much longer can I keep this up?

Despite the creative power and control that feed my sense of self and confidence; it creeped me out to realize I was becoming a hard-nosed CEO. My "management team members" were technically competent in their roles but they lacked good instinct or insight for business dealings. Every business-related matter rested on my shoulders. Everyone looked to me to lead them—and to feed them.

I suffered from a mix of challenges—some self-inflicted, some systemic, and some environmental. Generally speaking, I was confused about the difference between managing a business versus leading a business team. Thanks to Pops' guidance and a few of his "younger" business colleagues I discovered the "CLO-led" alternative to the traditional "CEO-run" method of running a business.

Earlier I mentioned the three charges of a CLO. I embrace these along with the ideal of *increasing wealth so everyone profits.*

As a CEO, this ideal meant one thing to me—make more money. I mistakenly equated financial independence with freedom.

As a CLO, however, the meaning of *increasing wealth so everyone* profits has matured into something, well, beautiful as a way of being in business. More on that later.

Words really matter. They carry history, meaning, and messages that define strategies, structures, systems, and culture. Semantics have strategic and tactical implications to the well-being of the business and its people. Our word choices and their substance determine if we're just working in or flourishing in business.

As a CEO my language as the leader was confused, therefore, my thinking was too. This meant my leadership and strategy resulted in muddied tactics and an action-impaired team. All of this dampened business performance.

Every line item on the income statement and every person putting their livelihood on the line working there is affected by my stewardship and leadership.

When the team members are confused, the customers are confused. When the customers are confused, the business suffers lower revenues due to fewer and harder sales, less repeat business, reduced goodwill, and lack of referrals. The customer experience is a lagging reflection on the leader's state of clarity.

In the vacuum of my "leadership," well-intended team members stepped up to fill in the gaps. It's called guessing. Such "initiative," while commendable, spawns ad hoc decision-making as well as individual and departmental silos. Such lack of integration amplifies inefficiencies. Interpersonal and interdepartmental battles ensue. As morale declines, profits are also depressed. That was my business.

Yet, I understood business to be a battle. My peer CEOs would often say with pride, "If it were easy, everyone would do it." We also embraced the lie that "Sales and operations are natural enemies"; and here, silly me, I thought we were all in one company.

There's an old saying that goes "You can't make a silk purse out of a sow's ear." Like many of my peer CEOs, I owned a collection of sow's ears and I was very committed to making silk purses.

Was it folly or hubris, or both? Perhaps this was the managerial equivalent of thinking the earth is flat? Unfortunately, nearly every CEO I knew or read about operated on generally the same plane of thought. We were a mutually indoctrinated and supportive admiration society excelling with the sameness of flawed language and a shallow understanding within a relatively unchallenged CEO ecosystem.

Sure, CEOs dominate the business landscape as the preferred title for the most senior officer in an organization.

Sure, running a business seems much easier when everything and every person is effectively reduced to a number on a financial spreadsheet or key performance indicator. But such a narrow focus is too risky and weak to sustain the long-term viability of the business and the well-being of the people.

This leadership laziness, and that's what it is, eventually depresses the profitability and promise of any business. Ironically, it's the exact opposite effect of what most CEOs are attempting to achieve. What starts as a way to organize the business inevitably results in a destructive pattern on so many levels. It was happening in my business.

The fallout from the CEO-system is real. In 2015, Gallup Consulting reported that *over half* of the employees surveyed are *not engaged* in their work. *One in six* employees are *actively disengaged*—think sabotaging the company. This means only about *one-third* of employees are *engaged* in their work.

This failing report card is cause for concern. There just can't be that many people on the planet who actually prefer being unhappily disengaged in their work!

We business leaders can do better, must do better if we're to compete today and tomorrow. Such an index of dread is an indictment of the CEO-system of management, not leadership. Business as we know it has a major systemic flaw and people, from the boardroom to the boiler room, are paying for it with their lives.

Lost in Place

Since the 1950s, the CEO-system is the dominant management model. CEOs, organizational charts, financial metrics, and human resources have grown in sophistication and automation to the point of near perfection ... in missing the mark. We're a CEO-generation lost in place, essentially a single path, old school way of working in an increasingly diverse and dynamic global marketplace. We're all doing business incompletely right.

My next statement is intended to alarm you. The CEO title screams "top officer driving the company into obsolescence." CEO is a neon sign of the nineteenth century Industrial Age mindset and method. My CEO colleagues are dinosaurs heading for extinction while mindlessly munching on the tops of trees as a new age is coming that will wipe them off the face of the earth.

We CEOs live in a time capsule that's out of touch with the business ecology and societal needs. We preach for innovation, but we're the last holdouts from it. Business is rotting from the head.

Chief Leadership Officer is the symbol and substance of the principles and practices of this century's organizational leadership and ways of being in business.

Looking Chris directly in the eyes, the CLO says, "You asked for the backstory. I told you; now what do you want to do? We can stop here and visit about the weather, family, and sports. Or do you want more about history, practices, and precepts of CLOs? Your call."

The CLO is definitely piquing your interest and scrambling your brain. Perhaps this is a CEO version of the movie *The Matrix*, where you've been languishing in some altered state while reality has been hidden. You're intrigued but unsure if the CLO is just some nonconforming idealist or a legitimate forerunner.

Chris says, "I'm game. And I'm assuming you're offering CLO as the alternative to the 'CEO-system' as you call it?"

The CLO says, "Yes. Chris, I came here to talk with you, and now your friend, about joining the conversation and collaboration of CLOs. Think of it as being more like an open source, co-creative community working to tap into the genius possessed by every person. For example, what companies like WordPress have done for internet website publishing and Firefox for web browsers, CLO is like that, but for business leadership."

You nod your agreement to Chris and the CLO to continue. Taking a sip of coffee you metaphorically agree to swallow "the red pill" with the hopes that you too can escape the matrix of management as you know it.

The CLO continues unfolding his backstory.

Chapter 3
Incompletely Right

You can't connect the dots looking forward; you can only
connect them looking backwards. So you have to trust that the
dots will somehow connect in your future. You have to trust
in something—your gut, destiny, life, karma, whatever. This
approach has never let me down,
and it has made all the difference in my life.

Stephen Jobs
Cofounder of Apple
1955–2011

CLO

Let's talk business and leadership history. Think of the
CEO-run system as a "method of management" that emerged
at the height of the Industrial Revolution in response to a
number of geopolitical, educational, societal, and business
climate factors. For simplicity, let's trace our way through the
pertinent highlights.

The title "CEO" is a relatively new term first used in the
mid-1950s. Previously, corporations were headed by Presidents
who often also carried the title Chairman of the Board. This
top company officer typically rose through the ranks of a
business and was promoted from *within* to the position of
President.

Birth of the B-School
The emergence of CEOs in the 1950s was rooted in a
significant educational investment beginning around the turn
of the 20th century. This would change the face and features of

business then and remains with us today. It was the creation of professional business schools. Their graduates would carry the doctrine and discipline of business through organizations in medicine, law, education, government, and so forth.

In 1881, The Wharton School of the University of Pennsylvania was founded to be a "School for Finance and Economy." This was the first business school in the USA. Wharton awarded its first Masters of Business Administration (MBA) in 1921.

In 1900, the Amos Tuck School of Business Administration and Finance at Dartmouth College opened to students. Graduates earned a Masters of Commercial Science (MCS) until 1953 when the degree shifted to an MBA.

In 1908, the Harvard Graduate School of Business Administration created the world's first MBA program. In 1922, Harvard created its doctoral business program and the *Harvard Business Review*.

The Touting of Taylorism

In those early years, all three b-schools shared a relationship with Frederick Winslow Taylor, a remarkably talented, highly connected, and diversely gifted man. The University of Pennsylvania awarded Taylor, a native of the Philadelphia area, an honorary degree as a Doctor of Science. He became a professor of management at the Amos Tuck School. The Harvard Graduate School of Business Administration based its MBA first year core curriculum on Frederick W. Taylor's highly regarded book *The Principles of Scientific Management*.

One can readily credit Taylor as being the inspirational and doctrinal father of business administration thought and curriculum. His thought leadership is so deeply embedded in the foundations to the most prominent and prestigious business schools of his day and today that his contribution is all but forgotten.

Taylor was born in 1856 and died in 1915. He first gained attention by applying engineering principles, such as time motion studies, to industrial production. Remarkably, many also credit Taylor as being the founding father of industrial engineering, management consulting, and technical training. His principles and processes guided the transformation of the US national economy from artisan guilds to assembly lines. As his methods spread so did the production capacity, productivity, and prosperity of a nation.

Seeking to increase shareholder returns, boards of directors sought out this elite talent pool to be company presidents. "Industry outsiders" were increasingly favored to effect the change. Disassociation with an industry and its people provided "professional distance" as a part of making "tough decisions," euphemisms for the heartless cuts and layoffs.

Prior to the 1950s, there is little record of the CEO title in use. Decades after the founding of business schools, their early graduates were reaching maturity, mass, and merit. As companies consolidated into conglomerates, the need arose for a high command and control person to whom the presidents of acquired companies or divisions would report. This "super-president" became known as the Chief Executive Officer.

By the mid-1970s, all but one of the Fortune 500 companies were headed by a CEO. This elite class of business person was richly rewarded for possessing a highly trained business mind to analyze and direct a business to meet and exceed shareholder returns.

In time, however, competition for top talent led to ill-conceived compensation packages and incentives. CEOs were rewarded for quarterly earnings and began to "manufacture" short term profits at the risk of long-term growth, sustainability, and human consequences. In the worst cases, ethical compromises would kill businesses such as what happened to Enron, WorldCom, and others.

For all the financial wealth creation of Taylorism, it

possessed an ugly downside of dehumanization. Before there were robots, there were people-bots. Workers on assembly lines were an input to production capacity measured almost exclusively in terms of financial output. What a person knew or could create mattered little. Assembly line output measured by speed and accuracy of repetition was the new standard of performance. A person's "value" was literally reduced to a production number with spirit- and mind-numbing effects.

Business became seen through the cold lens of a dashboard of metrics such as the P&L, earnings per share, return on investment, and market share. The "game of business" was born where Wall Street played and the rest of the world paid the price.

Taylor's Industrial Age methods and mindset are the forgotten gospel of general management theory and practice. They remain deeply embedded in the foundations of modern business. For well over a hundred years this original "management coding" intended for factory floor efficiency has been broadly applied.

In context, Taylor's work was as sound then as it is today. Unfortunately, it has been taken so far afield from its original intent, scale, scope, and use. In short, it is the misapplication of a profound set of operations and management principles being mistaken for leadership constructs and practices.

By the Numbers

Running a business principally by the numbers may be considered good management, but it is lazy, irresponsible, and incomplete leadership. Stuffing one's humanity in a compartment to justify "human sacrifices" on the altar of corporate profits and personal comp plan bonuses diminishes the very essence of what makes a business fully alive and successful.

In other words, business is being done "incompletely right." What is being done may be done very well, but there's this missing human element rendering it incomplete and underperforming.

Generations of CEOs, however, remain fixated and rewarded based on the financials, daily reports, stock prices, and production quotas. Stats provided a rationale for poor treatment of people and unreasonable demands. From the disconnected comfort of spreadsheets, it is far too easy to drive employees for ever greater increases in quotas, productivity, and profit margins without regard to what it takes to create it. Such numerical nearsightedness ultimately disadvantages the businesses from being its best.

Naturally, when employees are continually pressed to do more with less, cutting corners happens. Attention to details is compromised. Quality slips. Safety is risked. Every reasonable margin is squeezed right to the minimal edge of reasonableness. But "Whew, we made the numbers this month!" And that's all that matters, at least until the end of next month. Except, cut by cut the customer experience and brand equity start bleeding out.

The free market system rewards market efficiencies. In the Digital Age, people-bots are being replaced by real robots. Routine decision-making is being reduced to algorithms of artificial intelligence. Ironically, it is this centuries long season of dehumanization that is producing a new season where the uniquely human talent for invention, innovation, and creativity will be most valued.

We're entering the Age of Purpose and Meaning where the entirety of the person seeks to be more fully participating and connected to their work. More and more people want to know that their work matters and they've found a place to belong and to make a valued contribution beyond a paycheck. Quality of life increasingly matters.

Human Resources
Yet, how do we CEOs typically describe "our" people? We

use words like "human resources," "human capital," and "pieces of the puzzle." With all good intentions, we say things like "People are our company's greatest asset."

When we talk about people as "resources," "capital," and "assets," we reduce them to objects as if they are game pieces on a *Monopoly* board. People aren't property to be legally bought and sold. People aren't currency or things. Yet this is the normative CEO language and mindset. The reprehensible moral argument aside, such a subjugated view of people is just plain bad for business on so many levels.

People are refusing to be a cog in the wheels of industry. Thanks to the tech revolutions, we're in an era where people of all ages may more actively and affordably pursue their purpose and passion.

In short, the gig is up. The CEO-system is an obsolete business operating system unprepared to treat people as whole persons.

And that's why I needed to do something radically different in my thoughts, words, and actions. That's why being a Chief Leadership Officer is my departure from the old and my notice that we were doing business differently—more completely right.

After intently listening to the CLO, Chris turns, looks at you, and exclaims, "You know he's talking about us! We're CEOs! Mr. CLO says we have it all wrong." Mimicking the CLO, Chris says, "We each have our own 'little monsters' to feed and keep chained to our floors!" Looking at the CLO, he says, "Are you living on another planet? Business is business. Get with the program."

At this point, Chris's humor is a too thinly veiled defense of his ego. *Did he hear anything the CLO said?* The CLO's tone and talk are sensible and respectful, yet spiced with piercing conviction. Should you be insulted or appreciative?

Chris is posed for a cross-examination of the CLO. Chris is a gregarious and quick guy whose caustic tone is tempered by fiercely loyal friendship—often he's the loyal opposition just for the sheer joy of vigorous debate. Fortunately, Chris is spirited but not mean-spirited.

Winking at you, Chris turns to the CLO and with a false air of arrogance says, "Isn't my 7-series BMW, that *may be* taking you to the airport sooner than expected, ample evidence that I'm not doing it all that wrong?"

The CLO corrects, "I never said you had it 'all wrong.' Nor did Taylor. What you are is 'incompletely right.'"

A la the famous elevator scene in the movie *Jerry Maguire*, Chris made a dramatic but senseless flailing of his hands as if signing words. Chris verbalizes, "Then complete me!"

Intentionally rubbing his right eye with his right middle finger while looking at Chris, the CLO says, "I will."

Shaking his head from side to side, Chris says, "Man ... I relate to the good, bad, and ugly of running a business. For me it is really simple: make more money. Money seems to cover a world of problems."

"Ouch!" exclaims the CLO.

"Ouch, what?" asks Chris. "What's so wrong with making the big bucks? I mean, business is all about the money."

The CLO says, "The 'ouch' was about your statements that businesses only exist to make money and it covers a world of problems."

"Yeah, that's what business is all about."

"Chris," asks the CLO, "how much more money might you make if you didn't have to 'cover a world of problems?' What if all those problems are opportunities for growth and improvement?"

"Huh? You're kidding, right? Business is nothing but

solving problems: customers' problems, employee problems, financial problems, systems problems, problem, problems, problems. Money fixes my problems."

"No it doesn't," counters the CLO. "You said it yourself, it 'covers' your problems."

"Covers, fixes, whatever. Truth is, I'm the owner; if I don't beat the dollar drum then we're all out on the streets."

With a measured yet strong tone, the CLO says, "I agree that making a profit is essential to the health of the enterprise."

"Score one for me," exclaims Chris with a raised fist in victory.

The CLO says, "Just a second. Financial profit is the lifeblood of a business. Essential, but blood itself isn't life."

A confused Chris says, "I don't get it."

The CLO laughs at himself, "And Chris, at first I didn't get it either. I got into an argument with Pops one day about the fact that business only exists to make money. He told me I needed to learn the difference between being in business and doing business. He said I was 'all do' and 'no be.'"

"After that meeting, Pops arranged for me to meet Bob Scott, the namesake of the R. D. Scott Company, a large, international company. Pops promised that Bob could help me 'forge a better understanding of what it means to be in business.'"

"This was the beginning of truing my leadership mettle. As I was just about to leave Pops' place, he casually remarked, 'By the way, don't call him a CEO, he's a Chief Leadership Officer.' That was the first time I ever heard of a Chief Leadership Officer.

"Shortly after that meeting, I found myself sitting in Bob Scott's office. Wanna hear about it?"

"Absolutely," says Chris.

Chapter 4
Increasing Wealth

A business that makes nothing but money is a poor business.

Henry Ford
Founder of Ford Motor Company

CLO

Bob Scott welcomed me into his office. His reputation in the business community preceded him. Growing up I had heard my father and grandfather speak of him with high regard. Also, the R. D. Scott Company was known as a great place to work.

Bob was in his mid-to-late sixties and sported a full gray head of hair that betrayed his trim, youthful stride and even boyish looks. He said, "Your Pops is a legend whose life has touched many of us in the business community. What Taylor was to the Industrial Revolution, your Pops will be to your generation. Taylor was a man of his times, whereas your Pops is a person well ahead of his time. I'm so happy he's lived long enough to see the seeds he's sown for generations finally bearing fruit. You must be proud."

"Yes." I was proud to be Pops' great-grandchild but probably for different reasons than Bob was referencing. I didn't have a clue what he was talking about at that time.

Bob continued, "I was delighted when he called. And even more so when I heard you were his great-grandchild and he wanted me to meet with you so we could talk about *being* in business."

Bob's welcome was sincere, but in retrospect, my motives weren't so pure. I was there hoping to get some business out of this opportunity. Adding the R. D. Scott Company to my client list would be a big win for my company. It is rare to get fifteen minutes to pitch the top guy, let alone a full morning to build rapport and trust.

If listening to him talk about "being in business" for a few minutes was my price of admission, then so be it.

Bob began, "Your Pops filled me in on your open-ended conversation about doing business and being in business. It isn't an either/or, rather it is a both/and experience. *Doing* business amounts to the everyday activities such as managing, selling, production, accounting, customer service, and such.

"Micheal Gerber, the author of *The E-Myth*, popularized the concept of working in and on the business. Doing business is the same as his concept of working *in* the business. Working *on the business* is about the executive functions of improving the processes and systems.

"Standing on Taylor and Gerber's shoulders, Pops took it a step further. Being in business is a leadership role related to our conduct, ethic, and choices. Make sense?"

"Yes." Actually, this was making too much sense. I recognized I spent most of my time working in and on the business but I had no intention or time whatsoever invested in being in business. Oops!

"Good," Bob resumed. "Let's continue laying the foundation for being in business by asking a simple, yet pivotal question. Why does business, any business, exist?"

"That's easy, to make money. Everyone knows that," I blurted out.

Very matter-of-factly Bob informed me, "That's incompletely right."

I snickered, "I've been told I'm either completely wrong or completely right but never incompletely right. Seems like a contradiction."

Grinning, Bob said, "It's a more accurate and optimistic expression for a work-in-process, the glass being half full rather than half empty. It's partial credit for finding common ground. To tell someone they're completely wrong carries a high risk of offending a person and damaging the possibility for future progress. By acknowledging your answer as partially right, but incomplete, we're better able to engage in further dialogue."

"I like it. May I borrow that expression?"

"Please do," allowed Bob. "If you have children, try it with them."

He continued, "The question on the table is, Why does a business exist? You say it is to make money. So if that's incompletely right, then what's another way of saying, '... to make money?'"

"Uh ... to make a buck ... to make sales ... to make a profit?"

"OK. What does it mean 'to make a profit'?"

I answered, "A profit is what's left over after the expenses are paid."

"That's completely right for financial profit but still an incompletely right answer. What more can the noun *profit* mean beyond financial gain?"

"I don't know."

Bob coached, "Look it up on your phone."

Looking at my dictionary app I read, "A valuable return."

Bob asked, "Could 'a valuable return' mean more than money or economic benefit?"

"I guess, but aren't you slicing semantics at this point?"

"You're incompletely right again," Bob added. "The degree of difficulty for this question is high because we 21st-century business people have been raised to think of profit only in terms of money making as a financial measure. Such a shallow understanding, however, stunts business growth and, ironically, our profits.

"For example, within the narrow business sciences of economics and accounting your statement is completely right. But business first exists within a social construct—we in business hold a larger role in society. So *being in business* is about our very existence, our humanity, our reason for being. *Doing business* is our occupational role or the activities we do within the business."

His line of logic confounded me. "Bob, I kinda get that business needs to be bigger than making money. I can buy into the idea of some sort of 'social construct' whereby we're about improving the lot of our fellow members of the human race. But why does this matter to my small business? Right now, I am the social construct—survival of the fittest and all that Darwin stuff."

Bob said, "I'll answer you in two words, but promise please you'll keep an open mind for the rest of our conversation."

I agreed.

Bob stated, "All businesses exist to serve by Increasing Wealth."

Reacting instinctively, I let out a hissing and emphatic sigh, "S-s-semantics."

A good natured Bob teased, "So much for that open mind promise?"

"Forgive me," I said. "You set me up for some sort of Holy Grail moment and I get 'Increasing Wealth? Really? Making money. Earning profits. Increasing wealth. It's all the same."

"Open mind," reminded Bob.

"Yes, yes, of course," I reluctantly agreed.

Increasing Wealth

Bob explained, "The discipline of business exists to serve by Increasing Wealth. Think of 'Increasing Wealth' as the common 2-word purpose for every business—the reason for being (in business). Your company, my company, the company down the street have a shared purpose that is intended to inform how we are doing business and being in business while working on the businesses.

"Purpose is an untapped power buried beneath the busyness of our calendars spent on problems and meetings. This is why progress is so slow. We've not clarified our purpose so we can simplify the business in order to integrate purpose into every aspect of the business. We're so incompletely right that we keep trying to improve by working in and on the business, but we're never really being in the business."

Skeptically, I asked, "Is this Zen?"

Bob laughed, "It's about being more completely right."

"So you're telling me that the purpose of my business isn't making money but 'increasing wealth,' which sounds like a synonym to me."

"Before delving deeper into increasing wealth, let's do a small sidebar about the matter you just raised. The common purpose of all businesses is Increasing Wealth. Borrow that for the time being until you articulate a unique 2-word purpose statement specific to your business. That will sharpen the presence and practice for *being in business and doing business*, respectively.

"Okay, let's close that sidebar and return to it later. For now, let's get back to Increasing Wealth as the reason for why a business exists."

"Sounds great," I agreed.

"The word 'Increasing' implies ongoing action to become progressively greater in size, intensity, amount, number or degree. It's a commonly understood and applied word.

"Wealth is a word rich, pun intended, with meaning. Like profit, wealth is a word frequently debased to only mean financial abundance.

"Wealth is the state of being in weal, a little-used noun defined by Merriam-Webster as, 'a sound, healthy or prosperous state.' Weal, pronounced like 'wheel' and rhyming with peel, is an illuminating word. Well-being is a comparable contemporary word for weal as in the state or condition for a person to flourish and prosper.

"Wealth, therefore, is a more holistic state of well-being. You'll hear people refer to 'true wealth,' meaning more than one's financial condition. Weal is the whole of a person's or business's condition including—but not limited to— finances, relationships, vocation, body, mind, and spirit or whatever else one holds as dear to the heart."

Recognizing my earlier misstatement, I asked Bob, "Ah! So when I said, '... a business exists to make money' I was incompletely right. So if my most fundamental understanding of why a business exists is incompletely right from the start, then no matter how good we are at doing business we're not being in business. I'm screwed from the start. It's like a bad drive off the first tee in a game of golf. This makes total sense."

"Good," Bob said with a nod.

Specializing in Specialization

"Increasing Wealth matters in the larger social construct. Of the other sectors of society (for example, the arts, health, the environment, education, family, and government), the business sector generates the financial wealth that typically funds the others.

"Because increasing the wealth or the well-being of our society is our broadest duty, it is easy to get hyper-focused on the money part and leave out the people elements. Such a narrow or incomplete understanding of business as just 'making money' handicaps the strategy and business model. When the design of our businesses and the measure of our work is narrowed to financial measures, then we are as you now recognize completely incompletely right." He paused and then smiled at this turn of phrase to make sure I caught the subtle implications. Smiling back I indicated my understanding so Bob could continue his story.

"Frederick W. Taylor is the person who advocated specialization or division of labor into individual components and actions. His time motion studies were intended to remove waste from production in order to make a more prosperous company and workers. Let's give Taylor the benefit of the doubt that in his day he was intent on serving and improving society.

"Today, our business ecosystem is highly specialized far beyond Taylor's mills and factory floors. We see his influence in education, medicine, religion, law, sports, and more. It wasn't that long ago when a 'well-rounded person' was held in high regard. Today, it is almost seen as a losing formula. Instead of being well-rounded we're angular and directed toward a niche or specialty earlier in our lives, sports, careers, and businesses. There are pros and cons to this approach.

"For example, even weal has been specialized. The tax code allows for two basic forms or organizations: for-profit and not-for-profit. Charity used to be a virtue. Now it is part of one's financial plan for tax avoidance via deductions.

"Because not-for-profits were set aside to specifically address with society's challenges the unintended effect was business people were subtly granted license to be monetary mercenaries. So when agencies put their hats in their hands and beg, then we business people are supposed to fund their work by writing checks and donating volunteer hours.

"Given circumstances and for a variety of political and financial reasons, when government crosses lines and gets into the business of welfare, it further clouds and corrupts the role of business. In a free society and economy, charity is the moral imperative of the people, not the tax and legislative role of governments. The CEO-system reflects these realities."

Bob continued, "The holistic nature and pure elegance of the word weal has been chopped up, thrown under 'the wheels of progress,' and crushed beyond recognition. A reflection of our collectively compromised understanding of wealth is that we've lost our way. Society is dis-integrating and everyone pays the price! We wonder why the world is so harsh and difficult, even seemingly hopeless for so many. We in the business community have lost sight of why business exists in the first place. Over the generations, we've evolved to the point where we run our businesses with extraordinary professionalism and detail seeking market share, brand loyalty, financial gain, work-life balance, customer service, and more erroneously based on a deeply flawed understanding of the purpose of business."

"Metaphorically, you're saying CEOs are building businesses on sand instead of bedrock?"

"No. Businesses are indeed built on bedrock; it's just that the bedrock sits on a seismic fault line. Generations ago we stopped increasing wealth in order to just make more money. An economic earthquake is coming for CEOs and the businesses they run."

Chris halts the CLO, "Whoa, right there, partner. Look, I'm really enjoying the coffee, the wordsmith lessons, the historic sentimentality, geology, and all. What's that have to do with me doing business in this century in a dog-eat-dog fiercely competitive landscape? I can't afford to focus on somebody else's well-being halfway around the world or the San Andreas fault. I work in the here and now. I need every edge of advantage to keep my tenants paying their rent in full and on time so I can pay my bills and succeed.

"Let's cut the crap. We all know that in the end, it's all about the money, period. No money; no mission. And tomorrow, it will be the same as today only worse."

Respectfully hearing out Chris, the CLO says, "Interesting. You characterized the competitive landscape as getting 'worse.' Have you ever considered why and what you might do to make it better?"

Chris counters, "One person can't make a difference."

"Really," doubts the CLO. "Perhaps the point is being missed. What if I'm talking about integrating and shaping the future of your business so it is better positioned to compete and earn a higher profit as the leader in its chosen field? What if I'm showing you how to remove impediments to profitability? What if I'm working to prepare you for the future? What if I'm encouraging you to move away from the deep fault line and build on terra firma? What if you don't know what you don't know?

"Chris, with all due respect, you're stuck in the past running your business based on a 150-year-old plus business management and operating system, and you're lecturing me about being contemporary? Really? How long do you intend to remain an unconsciously stuck relic grounded in the management methods and mindset of the Industrial Age?"

An agitated Chris is somewhere between pissed and perplexed, but he holds his tongue.

The CLO defuses the building tension by asking, "You know I sincerely care about your well-being. Look, your skepticism is welcomed, but please listen, cross-examine me, and debate the issues. This banter is great. Ask your questions but, man, do yourself a favor. Hear me out, then form your opinion. Later today after you drop me off at the airport, feel free to drop this conversation, if that's what you choose to do.

"Recognize the signs of the times. There's a new day and a new way emerging in business. With it rises a new class of business leaders called Chief Leadership Officers who see the purpose of business is to be Increasing Wealth.

"In fact, once you understand the CLO-system for being in business, you'll recognize large companies that are already on this path. To make your choice, however, you need to be informed and open minded."

Being In Business
"More coffee, gents?" the barista asks.

"Yes, please ..." says Chris as he squints to read her name tag, "... Nala. That's a pretty name. *Lion King*, right?"

"Yes," she giggles, "My mother loved the movie. In Swahili, the name translates to 'gift, beloved, and successful.'"

"Nice!" Quick to take advantage of the needed diversion Chris gathered his thoughts and adroitly shifts the conversation to her, "By the way, Nala, this is really good coffee. What kind is it?"

Bubbling with enthusiasm she says, "Thanks! I'm so glad you like it. It's our special organic house blend from our Ethiopian fair trade coffee co-op. As I serve you here, together we're also serving villages in Africa. My parents immigrated from there."

There are no coincidences! Clearing your throat to swallow a snicker at Chris's expense, the CLO and you exchange knowing glances. Masterfully avoiding eye contact with either of you, Chris locks in on Nala. He stammers, "Your, ah, er, what'd you call it? Your 'fair trade coffee co-op?'"

"Yes, that's right."

"What's that about, Nala?" requests Chris.

"Thanks for asking. My husband and I started Latte Out Loud as a coffee bar and cafe to serve our local community and the world. We envisioned a place where families and neighbors gather, business persons meet, and people of all walks of life do life together. Seeing the three of you here deep in conversation is a joy. Please stay as long as you like. There's free WiFi if you need it."

Chris replies, "Thank you." Introducing us he points to the CLO, "This guy's an old friend visiting from Pittsburgh where we grew up together. *Go Black and Gold!* I live here now, as does he," pointing to you. "So what's the deal with this co-op thing?"

True to her name, a poised and confident Nala continues her story, "As business people, you'll appreciate that our business strategy includes investing part of our financial profits into several local agencies helping those in need. Internationally, we do the same for our Ethiopian growers. In fact, we're saving and raising money to go there to meet our co-op coffee growers. Several of our customers are going on this mission with us. We're so excited to meet our overseas production partners and their families and tour the farms and facilities. We'll take a bunch of photos and post them on social media and in the shop."

The CLO asks, "How goes your campaign?"

She points to a large graphic on the wall of a burlap coffee bag that is a fundraising thermometer. Across the top is written $25,000. She says, "We've been saving for two years to raise the money needed to make the trip and provide farming tools, educational materials, and other provisions. Our coffee bag is nearly full. We're $500 away from our goal!"

"That's cool," says Chris. His zany personality just couldn't let a kind word sit for too long. "I'll fair trade you my seat at this meeting for your serving tray. You'll probably benefit more from this meeting than I will." He stood and with a sweeping hand gesture and a gallant bow he offers Nala his chair. "I'll serve your customers until these two are through talking and when I have to take that guy," indicating the CLO, "to the airport."

Nala astutely senses an inside joke and wisely declines Chris's offer. Taking his seat, Chris told her, "Thanks for sharing your story about what your husband and you are doing here locally and abroad. These guys will tell you I needed to hear it. By the way, please add a slice of humble pie to my tab since I'm eating it and paying for it. Man am I paying for it," emphasizes Chris.

"We have cobbler but not humble pie. But, as you wish," she says, "the check is all yours."

Everyone chuckles. She smiles and returns to her duties behind the coffee bar. Turning to the CLO, Chris remarks, "That was well staged! She showed up right on cue."

Having eaten his humble pie, Chris is more attentive to the CLO's recollection of his Bob Scott meeting. The CLO picks up where he left off.

Chapter 5
Watch Your Mouth

"I am in the presence of the
Ghost of Christmas Yet To Come?" said Scrooge.
The Spirit answered not, but pointed onward with its hand.
"You are about to show me shadows of the things that have
not happened, but will happen in the time before us,"
Scrooge pursued. "Is that so, Spirit."

Charles Dickens
A Christmas Carol
1843

Bob Scott rhetorically asked, "What's the reputation of business in the media and popular culture?"

"Not good," I answered him. "The media almost uniformly portrays business people as greedy, heartless bastards who violate laws, abuse employees, and will sell our mothers if it can make an extra buck. The public has been brainwashed to view us like that."

Bob added, "All too often we hear phrases like, 'It's just business,' to excuse otherwise objectionable treatment of people or to bargain our ethical standards. Legions of compromised corporate employees dutifully bow to the god of greater shareholder returns. Enticed by salaries and benefits, people willingly opt for the soul-numbing 'security of a corporate job' in exchange for their limited time on earth."

"Bob, please stop," I pleaded. "That's such a negative view of business. I reject that! You're making it sound like every employment contract is a mini-deal with the devil. There are great companies who treat people right. Admittedly, there are some bad practices by CEOs. But most of us are like me—good people working to produce a good product at a fair price and striving to create a place where people can work hard and be rewarded fairly. I don't abuse people. In fact, I take care of my people."

Bob smiled, leaned back in his chair and observed, "No argument here. Let me ask, however, do you consider your last statement, 'I take care of my people,' to be a statement of management or leadership?"

What an odd question. I weighed my choices and answered, "Leadership. It's my job to take care of my people."

Bob said, "Do you think you could be incompletely right?"

"Sure. Tell me more."

"Your sincere interest toward your team members is leadership. But the words, 'I ... take care of my people,' is an insidious statement of mismanagement that's typical of well-intended but misguided CEOs. Think about it. Team members are not '*my* people' unless they're your children or kin—which they're not."

"C'mon now," I protested. "You're splitting hairs and putting words in my mouth. 'My people' is a term of endearment, as if they are my family."

"That's my point," Bob responded. "To 'care for them' is to put them *under* your parental supervision. Subjugating capable adults strokes the ego with a false sense of importance, even superiority. Such posturing undermines people and the business. You're subconsciously laying the groundwork for a bitter business rather than a better one."

"But some people want to be cared for," I argued.

Bob countered, "So you want weak, needy people to work for you?"

I replied, "Not really."

Bob continued, "On the spectrum of codependence, 'to care for them' is at best parental. In the middle, it is controlling. At its worst, it can turn abusive.

"Giving you the benefit of the doubt, you've assumed a parent–child or superior–subservient positional authority to define your relationship. You're the boss! This slippery slope creates a childlike class of followers seeking adult supervision. The implication is they're relatively incapable of it for themselves.

"Do you know what's worse?"

"What?" I asked.

"Over time, your employees will prove you right because that's the way of a management-run system. You recruited and hired them on the premise that they would be cared for. Your system of recruitment, screening, interviewing, employing, training, and rewarding is designed to 'care for them.' In fact, you're little more than a benevolent overlord who's preempting people from developing their inherent leadership capacity."

"Stop," I objected, "you're still putting words in my mouth."

An unwavering Bob pressed on, "Have you become so accustomed to your CEO idioms that you never considered their origin and what they truly convey? Words have meaning that create attitudes, get embedded in a culture, and have powerful consequences."

Bob's mincing of my words was so perturbing that I rechallenged him, "Then what's the CLO alternative? I'm sure you have one or two 'suggestions' for me." At this point, I was getting a bit testy.

Bob reminded, "The second charge of a Chief Leadership Officer is to position people to be leaders on and off their jobs. To do this means we want to associate through healthy adult-to-adult relationships with people who possess self-reliance and resilience—women and men with mettle.

"Leaders tend to bristle when treated like children. They wear personal responsibility proudly and often. *I'll take care of myself, thank you very much!* They generally seek collaborative partnerships of independent peers while avoiding codependent parental relationships which tend to be unhealthy for the business and the people involved."

"Sounds good in theory, but someone has to be in charge," I smugly objected.

"Absolutely!" Bob explained, "In a company of leaders everyone is in charge—of his or her work. Each leader has a clear sense of his or her scope of responsibilities and decision-making authority. When leaders interact, words such as trust, judgment, experience, and wisdom rise in importance over positional authority or title."

Trying to wrap my head around this, I told Bob, "Simplify it, please."

Bob smiled, "If we're all leaders-in-development, then the parent-child dysfunction shifts to an adult-to-adult dynamic. We're a team of peers with diverse experiences and backgrounds drawing upon one another versus falling in line behind the top dog—where the view too often describes the personality of the person 'leading' the pack."

The only experience I had anywhere close to this leader-to-leader description was with Pops, and now Bob. They shared a firm yet friendly manner that was assertive but not aggressive. They're tough and direct without making me feel stupid. They coach me into my best self-interest by giving me total control but sound advice for my decision-making.

Bob shared, "Far too many of my CEO colleagues whine, 'Why can't we find and hire more leaders?' I tell them to look in the mirror and admit they really want manager clones of themselves. Reflective of their middle name, CEOs are executives—managers and business administrators—not leaders."

"Whew," I whistled through pursed lips. "That's harsh. You're gonna tick off a lot of CEOs with talk like that."

"Ha," laughed Bob. "Truth does that, doesn't it?"

In a calm, professorial voice he asked, "Is it harsh to pen

people into stalls like animals? Oops, excuse me, you call them human resources in cubicles," he sarcastically jested. "I find little joy in corralling and controlling my teammates. It exhausts and exasperates all of us while festering counterproductive bitterness. It also undermines the real work at hand that goes into our increasing wealth enterprise.

"In contrast to power and control, there's being an influencer of leaders. A person growing as a leader is freer and more true to who they are.

"Given your words, 'I take care of my people,' please tell me which of us is the more harsh? Which of us is leading? Which of us is increasing the state of weal?"

Bob challenged my assumption, yet even in vigorous debate, he dignified me. As his mother taught him, he was good at watching his mouth.

"Bam," blurts Chris. "He didn't dignify you; he owned you!" The lesson on watching one's mouth, was apparently lost on Chris.

Unruffled the CLO matter-of-factly reframes Chris's correction, "Technically, a CLO would never 'own' another person."

"Touché Mr. CLO," quips Chris.

Awarded the point, the CLO continues, "Bob drew distinct lines between leadership and management. Previously I tended to use them almost synonymous.

I've developed a habit of asking myself, *Am I managing or leading? Am I doing business or being in business?* Candidly, being a boss is easier for me but tougher on team member development. Once I go down the bossing lane, it's hard to reverse it.

Leading means resisting the temptation for expediency.

With practice, my mastery in leading translates into a better, more fluid workplace for the team."

Unmasking Management

Almost as an afterthought, the CLO says, "Bob told me something that still haunts me. Did you know that an archaic definition of management is trickery or deceit? More along the lines of manipulation or controlling objects to one's personal gain at the expense of others."

"Really?" Chris asks.

"Bob and I speculate that at some point in the early days of the Industrial Revolution workers secretly tagged conniving supervisors and owners as 'management' because of their unscrupulous manner and mistreatment of people. The derogatory reference to 'management' was so aptly descriptive that it stuck. Generations since, management became so commonly descriptive that it gained legitimacy to mean the people in charge of controlling things, processes, projects, and people. Today, the original meaning and context are long since lost, but so telling."

"Amazing!" lets out Chris.

The CLO proposes, "The joke is on us, but it's not a laughing matter. The c-suite, managers, and supervisors are identified as 'line management.' Cartoonist Scott Adams created *Dilbert* and built a media empire by cynically poking fun at our convoluted ways, dysfunction, and manipulation.

"It's easy to rely on 'management techniques' while giving lip service to actual leadership development. We think we're cleverly doing right when we're actually sowing seeds of distrust and division. The more I pay attention to what my CEO peers say and post in business blogs, journals, and publications, the more disturbed I become at the callous disrespect with which we treat 'our people' in the narrow, 'noble' pursuit of financial profit at all costs.

"Our words betray an ingrained attitude of superiority and

disparagement that's essentially based on a hierarchal position. 'Man's inhumanity to man' is an institutional disregard for personhood justified in the name of 'I'm just doing my job.'

"It takes soul-separating to behave in this manner."

"Soul-separating?"

"The favored, euphemistic term is to 'compartmentalize' or draw an artificial line between one's life and work in order to make 'better business decisions.' This gives space and a rationale for the objectification of people as assets, resources, or pieces.

"The CEO-approach is increasingly inept and unable to compete so it is less tolerated by people with options. Company fortunes have been built on the basis of soul-separating and the churning and burning out of people. Even when such Faustian practices are beautifully gift wrapped with benefits packages and golden handcuffs there are consequences. Hell must be paid."

Chris asks, "Geez, you make us CEOs out to be real a-holes. So what do we do about it?"

The CLO responds, "It starts at the top of any organization—the board, CEO, and c-suite. Someone has to raise a hand and say, 'We're capable of being better than this.'"

"But what do we actually do?" Chris asks.

The CLO says, "Start with a clear definition of the purpose of the organization and build alignment from there in the strategy, structure, and systems. Think more holistically about being in business and creating a return to stakeholders, not just a return to shareholders. When in doubt ask yourself if you're increasing wealth or not."

"Huh? In English please," Chris asks.

"Our cafe owners personify this. Nala and her husband buy their coffee beans from fair trade partners, creating awareness and opportunities for others to participate whether it is buying a cup of coffee or going on their Ethiopian excursion. This coffee shop is their platform for serving people locally and worldwide while providing for themselves.

"They defy CEO business 'logic' which breaks down every decision to money and productivity metrics. And as important as those analytics are, when they rule, it's a sure sign a business is in an executive-induced decline. As CEOs, we're addicted to the money and largely in denial about it."

Chris pressed, "But how did you start making your change from manager to leader?"

"I started by taking my mom's advice to watch my mouth. Listening to my words and expressions, I shockingly discovered what I said and did were miles apart from my beliefs. My words conveyed previously unchallenged attitudes and assumptions common to the CEO parlance that undermines relationships. I didn't walk my talk and my break in personal integrity was painfully apparent. Worse, my ineffective and destructive talk was mimicked and amplified by team members.

The Dance of Deception

"The result is that 'management and labor' have devised an mutually deceptive dance and language of destruction based on blaming the other party. What a sick system!

"The adverse business effects are so dear. Loss of operational productivity, under-delivery with customers, turnover of talented people, and quality issues are just some of the costly effects. Every line on the company financial statements is negatively impacted. I estimate our sales and profits are depressed by at least twenty-five percent.

"There had to be a better way to do and be in business; but I only knew one way—the CEO-system.

"Keep talking," Chris encourages; "this is hitting eerily close to home."

"For generations, we've been indoctrinated in the Industrial Age game of financial profit maximization. It's a divisive win–lose doctrine.

"The classic example is management and labor union relationships. Long after contracts are settled, emotions are not. What few seeds of trust remain are crushed underfoot by the weight of the residual mutual cynicism. The flaws are costly to the business plus it divides society into feuding classes. Ironically, this fully extended arms-length way of doing business is so wasteful that it actually depresses financial profit.

"Today, such a single-minded pursuit of financial profit maximization is eroding the societal landscape and causing a consumer backlash. More and more it is being revealed as the losing strategy it is."

Chris notices, "This really haunts you."

"Yes. The underlying decay is rotting our social and moral fabric. Such human toll is avoidable and the economic waste is unnecessary.

"Bob was right. I was managing, not leading, but I thought I was a leader. By my omissions, I was the more harsh person. His striking contrast shook me from the slumber of my CEO airs and errors."

Chris asks, "You said there had to be a better way. Is this CLO approach a source of hope?"

The CLO says, "No 'thing' is a source of the hope. You want hope?" Gesturing around the cafe like a tour guide, the CLO instructed, "Look around this place. You met and heard Nala, our barista, effervesce about the purpose of this business? Isn't her hope palpable? Yet, do you question her professionalism toward her coffee craft and business operations? Have you noticed her upbeat, energetic step as she serves? Do you get that she's bringing high expression to who she is? She exudes hope.

"Hope only exists in the human spirit. CLOs respectfully steward, harness, and hone the vagueness of hope into a more specific, organized, cohesive, and contributing whole. That's a huge responsibility and calling. And when we get it completely right, it goes very right.

"Our coffee shop owners are instinctively Chief Leadership Officers. They personify the entrepreneurial trend of solo owners who opt-out of the traditional job market to pursue a meaningfully integrated life and work. Latte Out Loud is their mission. Through every cup of coffee, they give expression to who they are, what they envision, what they enjoy and value. It's their contribution to making the world a better place.

"CLOs work with people, not through them. We're maximizing purpose in order to profit people in the most robust sense of the word profit.

"The CLO-system confounds and disturbs the CEO psyche because it runs counter to generations-long, deeply held norms and understanding. Admittedly, The CEO-system has done so much to improve the quality of life of so many people. 'Why risk changing it?' That's the scary, obvious objection I repeatedly hear.

"The world has changed! The old ways were wrong from the start but produced so much gain that it was an accepted cost of doing business. Like frogs in the kettle, we've gradually been warmed into complicit complacency at the expense of our standards of wealth.

"We pay with our intangible weal in order to gain material goods. In return, we're stressed out, burned out, bummed out, addicted, mindlessly entertained, overweight, disabled, and dying prematurely because we're more afraid of what's outside the soon-to-be-boiling pot than the current cost of staying put. It is inevitable that the CEO-run system will boil. We happen to be at that place in history where the temperature of the business climate is dramatically rising."

Chris chimes in, "I see where you're going with this. It's the remake of *A Tale of Two Cities*. When I was in an English Literature class we read it and had to memorize the opening sentence:

It was the best of times, it was the worst of times, it was the age of wisdom, it was the age of foolishness, it was the epoch of belief, it was the epoch of incredulity, it was the season of Light, it was the season of Darkness, it was the spring of hope, it was the winter of despair, we had everything before us, we had nothing before us, we were all going direct to Heaven, we were all going direct the other way—in short, the period was so far like the present period, that some of its noisiest authorities insisted on its being received, for good or for evil, in the superlative degree of comparison only.

Chris continues, "Today we have big screen TVs, smartphones, autonomous cars, medical care, and multiple grocery stores within a two-mile radius of our heated and cooled homes. Our basic needs and creature comforts are readily met. But too many of us are addicted to illegal drugs, overly-prescribed to legal ones, or self-medicating with chocolate. Our lives are dis-integrating before our eyes, yet we feel helplessly caught up and unable to escape the daily grind. We toil to fund our basic necessities while indulging in therapeutic shopping, entertainment, sports, and other distractions. We comfortably suffer in the symptoms of compartmentalized meaninglessness."

Chris relates it back to the CLO. "When you blurted your true feelings to your Pops, you spoke for many of us who are asking, 'Is this as good as it gets? Where's the joy? Where's the peace?' We really are in the best of times, and in the worst of times. So Mr. CLO, what the hell do we do about our declining standard of wealth?"

Soul-Sourcing

The CLO says, "Today, we can do better because we know better about how to be better. Instead of soul-separating, CLOs are soul-sourcing. We want whole relationships and whole persons who are leading their lives by living from their soul through their purpose with passion, energy, and smarts.

"Each person possesses an innate desire to make a positive difference. That's the soul's cry inviting us to be better leaders of our lives and to make our lives count. CLOs facilitate people being more fully present and meaningfully engaged in a worthwhile, intelligent, and profitable expression of their purpose and hope. It's a better way to be in life which makes it a better way to be in business."

Chris asks, "Okay. So where are all the leaders then?"

The CLO says, "They're everywhere, but they're undeveloped. Leaders are both born *and* made. Every person is born to be a leader of his or her life. Yet there's a dearth of leaders across the world because leadership is also a learned skill. Sadly, most of us have only been taught how to minimally manage our lives, let alone lead them. It is also why CLOs position people to be leaders in their lives and work. It's the old saying, 'A rising tide lifts all boats.'

"Candidly, before I was a CLO, I would have disparaged the Latte Out Loud coffee shop owners as dreamers and written them off as fashionable do-gooders. Actually, they're evidence or a case study for the future of small and big business. Pay attention and learn. They're pioneering what it means to be on-purpose and to master the art of raising the standards of living and of wealth. They're the future in more ways than we might believe possible.

"Now, imagine their hope, heart, and passion for what they're doing being fully partnered with the talent, disciplines, and experiences of a CEO. That's what a Chief Leadership Officer seeks to accomplish—an integrated, more full-bodied living and work experience organized to make a world of difference."

Chris looks at you while nodding his head and cautiously says, "I'm beginning to believe it's plausible to be completely right."

Chapter 6
An Interest in Self-Interest

As one digs deeper into the
national character of the Americans,
one sees that they have sought
the value of everything in this world
only in the answer to this single question:
how much money will it bring in?

Alexis de Tocqueville
French Historian
1805–1859

CLO

Bob Scott made his point to me: the empty toil of the Industrial Age included a high cost to weal that was largely hidden by a broadly rising standard of living. People were willing to "sacrifice" so their family could experience "The American Dream." The cost-benefit was accepted based on the hope of one's children being materially better off than their parents. For its time, it made sense to the collective conscience.

The Digital Age, however, shifted the dynamics of production from laborers to "thought workers" whose intellectual output surpassed the manual work value of prior generations. The rise of robotics and artificial intelligence are massive technological disruptors with implications to the standards of living and wealth.

Despite these socioeconomic megatrends, the gulf of distrust between management and labor remains. The cosmetics of the relationship are improved but it is still lipstick on a pig. Corporate systems, structures, and mentalities remain rooted in a management mode relatively unchanged at its core. The economics of competing and succeeding in the marketplace with an "us and them" divided house mentality is invariably increasing expensive.

Bob told me, "CEOs will face increasing difficulties trying to out-manage a corporate culture rooted in division. Excessive tangible expenses in people turnover, quality issues, customer service, and such will sink them. Intangible costs such as losses in brand equity and reputation will exasperate the matter. Management's greater efforts to control these costs by edicts will only widen the divide of mutual discontent.

"The dominance of the hierarchal, command and control, traditional corporate approach is out of touch with people's self-interest and purchasing preferences. If a company treats its employees like dirt, then the word on the web is spread at the push of a button. Review sites abound in every facet of the business from products, customer experiences, working conditions, pay scale, benefits—you name it and it can likely be found. This high degree of transparency and stakeholder accountability scrambles the CEO business model.

"For top corporate officers, we can either fight it or fight for it. CLOs fight for it! We take this different tact from our CEO peers because we have a different operating system, if you will, that views such openness as healthy."

A woman with a to-go coffee cup in her hand approaches the table. Looking at the CLO she brightly exclaims, "Excuse me gentlemen for interrupting, but I can't believe my eyes, *it is you!*" The CLO's eyes brightened in recognition and he stood to greet her with a cordial hug. After a few pleasantries, he introduces her as Cheryl, also a CLO.

In a quiet aside to you Chris jests, "This is getting weird, fast—two CLOs in the same day. Who would have thought it was possible?"

Cheryl says to the CLO, "I'm so disappointed I missed your talk this morning. Word travels fast. A couple of others posted a few of your choice quotes on their social media and reported how much they learned at the chapter meeting."

Cupping his hand to his mouth and leaning in toward us, Chris wisecracks with a whisper, "My God! There's more of them!"

Unaware of Chris's shenanigans, Cheryl explains her absence to the CLO. "Our production team leader's wife died late last night of breast cancer. We knew she was close but the timing of her death caught us all by surprise. He called me with the news in the wee hours of the morning. I've been with his family and him since to console and mobilize our team's support. With my schedule shuffled, I missed you this morning.

"But, I'm so fortunate to bump into you here!"

Despite her circumstances, this impromptu reunion is clearly a happy coincidence for Cheryl and the CLO. Turning to the two of you, the CLO further introduces Cheryl as the CLO of a medical device manufacturing business with over a hundred team members. A couple of years ago they met at a CLO Summit and remained in touch since.

Cheryl says to us, "Please forgive me for barging in, but I just had to say hello."

The CLO says, "I see you've got a to-go cup. Do you have a few minutes to stay? We were just talking about being a CLO. Would you invest a few minutes and share your story?"

Checking the time on her phone, she says, "I'm headed to an appointment but yes. I've ten minutes. Given my early morning wake-up call, I needed a jolt of java in my system. Latte Out Loud brews the bee-s-s-st coffee."

Chris chimes in, "Your fellow CLO was about to make the case for why CLOs embrace transparency compared to CEOs.

Did I characterize that right?"

"Yes, Chris," says the CLO. "Cheryl, what's your take on the benefits of such openness?"

She chuckles, "'Transparency' is CEO code or a euphemism for, 'we really don't want you to know this nor do we think you have much to add to it. So, we'll tell you just a few more of our 'secrets' than we did before.'

"Transparency isn't a doing-thing that a leader can turn on and off like a television set. It is an attitude and posture toward others, a way of being in business. Plus, if we think there are actually company secrets, then we're delusional. Team members are smart and are more in touch with the day-to-day business than we are. In fact, when I was a CEO, the team was usually waiting for me to catch up with them. I was the one lagging them," she quips about herself.

Cheryl shares, "These half-measured attempts at being more transparent, ostensibly to build trust, have just the opposite effect. They create the appearance of something bigger being hidden and only serve to invite stakeholders to imaginatively fill in the gaps with conjecture that leads to rumors and misinformation.

"That's why we're an open-book business. When team members have the facts, then we're more consistently based in reality."

Addressing Chris and you, she asks "Do you feel like you have constant communication problems in your businesses? Some times, very costly ones at that?"

Nodding our heads in agreement, Chris adds, "Absolutely."

Cheryl resumes, "As a CLO, I welcome a free flow of internal information with almost no exceptions. This is what respecting adults do with and for each other. We speak candidly to build trust, eliminate problems, improve the workplace, and increase productivity. We're one team, not opposing sides as the traditional management–labor relationship seems to be portrayed. We're a team battling together to right wrongs in our chosen field of medical devices.

"Withholding information from the rest of the team and vice versa muddies the waters. Information is power. In my CEO days, I mistakenly held onto information for power and control. All I did was disadvantage the team, business, and myself; other than that, 'it worked well,'" she says with air quotes and a roll of her eyes.

"An open and real dialogue based on facts and truthfulness lays a foundation for trust. And when things do go wrong, then there's a greater possibility for a more rapid and accurate recovery. And things will go wrong," she says as she clasps her hands together, throws them in the air, and simulates an explosion, "Kaboom."

Authenticity

Chris jumps in, "First, my condolences for the loss at your team. You've really rallied the team. Second, given all the transparency and the altruism you're doing for your employees it sounds like that policy is really working."

"Cheryl," the CLO resumes, "in these few remaining minutes we with have with you, what's your take on Chris's observation about, 'the transparency and the altruism you're doing for your employees.'"

She obliges the CLO, "We're one team with many different members each leading in our respective roles and responsibilities. When one member of our team suffers we all suffer, and the business suffers.

"Admittedly as the CLO, I'm a more visible member of the team with a larger scale and scope of responsibilities, but still I'm just a member of the team. CLOs don't *do* transparency and altruism as if we're putting on and taking off clothing. We *are* transparency and altruism. No put-ons here.

"When I was a CEO I had my feel-good initiatives and compliance trainings on programs like trust, diversity, work-life balance, wellness, transparency, sexual harassment, and more. For all the value and importance of these initiatives, every time we sprinkled this 'magic dust' over the 'employees' we patted ourselves on the back for all the good we were doing. We were fooling ourselves. We had a sincere surface 'commitment' with no real backing, intention, or time to actually implement. We offered the programs, earned the merit badges, and moved on to business as normal.

"The team saw through it for what it was—disingenuous accessorizing. The depth of our sincerity was self-interested legal compliance and liability mitigation. They knew it. Heck, we knew it, but it was the way the game was played. Such CEO optics and an avatar-like 'leadership' style reinforced our differences.

"With all due respect, playing 'the role' is a big part of why CEOs are relics. We get sucked into becoming pretentious posers who check their humanity at the door in favor of an earning per share uptick. We start off 'faking it until we're making it,' except we never stop faking it. Thankfully, that inauthenticity doesn't play well in today's marketplace."

Picking up on Chris's rascally ways, she asks, "Hey Chief, you getting this?"

With large, slow rhythmic nods of his head, Chris says, "Wow! Am I ever. I'm thinking of selling my business and going to work for you."

Immediately she jabs back, "No! We're not hiring."

Everyone gives a good natured laugh. Chris has a worthy verbal volleyer.

"Truthfully, I'm impressed," compliments Chris. Never being one to let a nice word sit for too long, however, he punches back, "But Ms. CLO, is your game as good as your talk?"

Wise enough to not take his bait, she humorously rolls her eyes in the CLO's direction and comments, *"That is* a CEO asking me that question, right? Patience, right?"

Chris smiles and concedes, "Okay. Your point. But really,

how does one get started with this CLO stuff?"

She really has Chris's number. Cheryl asks, "Chris, why are you asking me that question? You already know the answer."

With every reply, she keeps winning over Chris. A now chuckling Chris turns to the CLO and says, "Where did you find her? She's amazing."

Looking back to Cheryl, Chris says, "You're right. It starts with me, doesn't it? Remember, I'm still learning this CLO stuff and *in all transparency*, I'm really skeptical. So cut me some slack. I don't share your experience with this CLO shtick."

Cheryl says, "Knowing the guy sitting next to you," referring to the CLO, "you'll know a whole lot more by the time you leave Latte Out Loud. He's one of the best CLOs there is."

The CLO nods once to acknowledge her kind praise.

Returning to Chris, she confirms, "You're right. It starts with deciding you want to be a better leader and the leader of a company of leaders. That means letting go of all the posturing. The decision to go from being a CEO to a CLO is a tough shift but a worthy and profitable one. Do your heart and head work and you'll better know who you really are."

"So this is top-down?" asks Chris.

"In an existing business it has to start top-down. The CEO is the only person in a position to effect a company wide transition and forge a team.

"As CLOs we're *in* authority, but we're not *the* authority. Once we let go of having to be the authority, then team members can rise to be authorities in their respective positions and perspectives. To create trust, give trust."

"That's wise," adds Chris. "Not my forte," he jokes.

"I see that," quips Cheryl, "but it is in your self-interest."

"Really? How so?"

"The business will run better, faster, more efficiently, and more profitably. Mark my words, get that old school gunk out of the engine of your enterprise and watch what happens when all that pent-up talent is released.

"I've observed a fascinating phenomenon on the other side of the transition. Gone is the top-down, bottom-up hierarchal organizational direction. Instead our movement is left to right, symbolic of the team's unity in forward momentum and progress. Everyone profits in a forward and onward vector."

Ever the quick study, Chris begins filling in the logistics, "So it starts with me, goes to my c-suite, probably my managers and supervisors, then the rest of the team, right?"

"Yes."

Chris shares, "Turning the company 180 degrees seems like a daunting and disciplined task. I have to wonder if I have the discipline to stick through it."

Cheryl lets out a laugh. "You're incompletely right. You only have to turn the business 90 degrees from top-down to left-to-right. Don't make it out harder to be than what it is. Leverage what you're already doing right and reform what needs to be improved." With a fencer's thrust of her index finger toward Chris's heart, she playfully says, "And it starts with you, Mr. CEO. Lose that title!"

Chris grasps his heart as if struck by her verbal lunge.

The CLO intercedes, "Chris, you've proven you have ample discipline to run a business. Now you just need a system that leverages your existing discipline. Just like college or law school, take it in small, consistent steps and you'll eventually 'graduate' as a CLO."

"Wait," says Cheryl. "He's a lawyer! That explains a lot. Why didn't you tell me I was helping a—"

"Stop!" says Chris abruptly cutting her off. "Spare me the lawyer jokes. Since I became a real estate developer, I'm in recovery."

Cheryl ribs him, "Oh man, I've got some doozies too."

The CLO steps in to referee the conversation, "Cheryl, earlier you mentioned self-interest. Elaborate on that please?"

Self-Interest

"Sure. Self-interest is a good thing. Self-interest is a bad thing. We're all self-interested. It motivates us. We're prone to act when things are in our interest. We can't lose sight of self-interest, yet we can't let it hinder our leadership either.

"For example, as a mom, when I act in the self-interest of my children I'm ultimately acting in my self-interest. I want the best for them which, for this example, I define as self-reliance. But if I become a helicopter or tiger mom, then I stifle their growth and development and diminish my self-interest.

"Self-interest must be tempered by perspective and wisdom. Coming to terms with self-interest and honing it into productive action is one of the finer arts of being a leader of oneself and others. That's why the 'Everyone Profits' value is so relevant to CLOs. The 'everyone' part of this expression includes me. It's not always an easy integration, but it is always necessary to check in with one's self-interest.

"Every business transaction is a self-interested exchange between the parties. It doesn't matter if it is a sales contract or an employment agreement; both parties are acting in their self-interest. The business of business is anchored in having trusted relationships. Transactions generate sales, but relationships create profits. That's how I see it."

The CLO says, "Cheryl, thanks for your insights."

"A lot of mistakes are behind learning these lessons," Cheryl confesses. "I hope they'll help."

The CLO digs further, "So Cheryl, how do you mutually align self-interests, especially conflicting self-interests?"

"Whew," she exhales, "I don't have time today to answer that question. And even then, there are no guarantees for alignment.

"Nevertheless, I start by looking for common ground. This means I have to know the good, bad, and ugly of my self-interest. Then I need to explore with questions about another person's self-interest. Then, we compare the two and see what can be done in the overlap so everyone profits. If we don't overlap with purpose, then both parties walk away better knowing why, which is important.

"When parties are mutually aligned around a common purpose such as Increasing Wealth, we're better at letting go of our individual self-interests and joining forces. For example, we market and position our business in our self-interest by targeting the work and customers we most want. When we're in front of those select prospects, then our self-interest is substantially served. This means we're that far freer to serve and 'sell' in the prospects of self-interest. We can play with abandon."

Chris asks, "So you're saying that part of leadership is self-interest and personal responsibility working hand in hand?"

"Yes. Returning to my prospective customer example, when we're the right people in the right place with the right customers we can be trusted advisors rather than convincers or hard closers. There's nothing better than letting go and serving in the best interests of our customers. We'll earn our fair share of the business. Our lack of pretense and innate confidence is remarkably liberating."

Chris adds, "Yeah, but getting to that point of trust is the hard part."

"True," she agrees. "But the common purpose discussion opens the door for building such trust."

"So you win the business, then what?"

"Easy," she says, "We have to deliver on the customer journey from sales to service and beyond. The most sincere, selfless, and knowledgeable trusted advisor will be undermined if the business support systems and people don't back her up with delivery. It is a total team effort."

Chris says, "What I hear you saying is that the total customer experience weighs in the minds of customers and clients more than ever."

"That's right, Chris. Traditionally, businesses have focused on the direct customer experience but largely ignored the indirect customers and stakeholders. Both are increasingly important factors in the decision-making process for engaging prospects and retaining customers."

Stake and Chain

Turning to the CLO, she asks, "Have they learned about stakeholders and the 'Customer Chain' yet?"

"Go for it," encourages the CLO.

"Okay."

Cheryl says, "Businesses used to be able to succeed in relative obscurity. Customers didn't pay any attention to the supply chain or sourcing of their goods and services. For example, whether their eggs were caged, free range, farm fresh, cage free, organic, or something else, they didn't differentiate. Increasingly, people care about these matters for a variety of self-interested reasons ranging from personal health to animal treatment to working conditions and others.

"Across every industry, this level of corporate accountability and scrutiny is only increasing in importance. It has been brought on by the public acting in their self-interest in a free market capitalism. This fundamental shift in the profit equation is an extraordinary return to the weal of people and the planet—unparalleled opportunities for businesses to serve and prosper thanks to this more comprehensive demand by certain customer segments.

Chris proposes, "So the CLO approach is economics, not altruism? It just makes more sense to do right by doing good."

"Right on, Chief," says Cheryl. "CLOs are the future. We're coming out of an era where rampant managerial malfeasance was rewarded rather than readily punished. The ever present stress 'to make our numbers' by whatever means necessary is a corrupting influence. Cutting corners in order to trigger bonuses and profit sharing took self-interest to the extreme of win–lose, and business has been disintegrating in reputation since.

"For generations we've heard, 'caveat emptor' or buyer beware as a warning to consumers. The watchword today is, 'caveat venditor' or seller beware. How you do business is being watched, recorded, reported, and posted. Buyers have social media networks with a powerful reach."

The CLO says, "Think back to our discussion about being incompletely right. CLOs are doing business more completely right—making consistent progress toward integrity. We view self-interest in a free enterprise private economy to be like nuclear energy. Here's an unlimited, positive, intrinsic motivator of people waiting to be set free and wisely guided into productive use until they're free to lead themselves. That's what leaders do. That's what CLOs do to transform the corporate culture so it is heavy on leaders working in a unified self-interest employing solid business practices to profitable ends."

Chris says, "Sounds good to me. How does this work?"

The CLO laughs, "That's ironic! I asked Bob a similar question."

Cheryl says, "Gentlemen, I really need to leave for my appointment. It's been a pleasure."

Cheryl hugs the CLO and shakes hands. After she leaves, the CLO says, "Okay, next let me share what Bob taught me about unity through team engagement."

Chapter 7
Team Engagement

The NBA is never just a business.
It's always business. It's always personal.
All good businesses are personal.
The best businesses are very personal.

Mark Cuban
Owner of the Dallas Mavericks NBA Franchise

CLO

Drawing comparisons from CEOs to CLOs was helpful so I asked, "Bob, how else do CLOs do business differently from CEOs?"

He answered. "We seek integrity—unity and constancy of purpose along three measures or what we call the 3Es: Engagement, Efficiency, and Effectiveness. Peter Drucker, the management guru, famously said, 'Efficiency is doing things right; effectiveness is doing the right things.' Most successful businesses manage with these two dimensions. Engagement adds a third, people-oriented dimension."

"What did Professor Drucker say about Engagement?"

"He didn't specifically, but I will," offered Bob. "Engagement is being right with people. Note the verb shift with engagement to 'being' whereas efficiency and effectiveness are 'doing' actions."

"Bob, but 'being right with people' is subjective?"

"True. Therefore, objective measures are used. Gallup has done extraordinary work in the area of employee and customer engagement." Bob said. "Please open up the Gallup website on your phone, look up 'employee engagement,' scan it, and then tell me what you learn."

With a quick search and scan, I reported, "First, they have validated methods to assess employee and customer engagement. Gallup defines 'engaged employees' as 'those who are involved in, enthusiastic about, and committed to their work and workplace.'"

Continuing to scan the website, I let out, "Whoa! Their 'meta-analysis shows that business units in the top quartile of employee engagement are 17% more productive, suffer 70% fewer safety incidents, experience 41% less absenteeism, have 10% better customer ratings, and are 21% more profitable compared with business units in the bottom quartile.' That's a huge difference in profitability!"

"Keep looking," Bob encouraged.

My jaw dropped as I read aloud, "Gallup has been tracking this for 30 years by researching over 30 million employees! That's impressive."

"And," Bob led me, "keep scanning."

"87% of employees worldwide are not engaged in their work. 87%! That's depressing."

"But what do they say about companies with highly engaged workforces?"

"That quartile outperforms their peers by 147%."

Bob said, "Let's talk big picture. The surveyed companies are operating efficiently and effectively enough to produce a financial profit, but they're not engaging people. Agreed?"

"Yes," I concurred.

Bob resumed, "Now that you have a sense of the opportunity cost and potential gains, ask yourself what's going on systemically? How is it that only 13% of the employees surveyed worldwide are engaged in their work?"

My thoughts were swirling with this marketplace reality check. *How could 87% of employees not be engaged in their work? How desperate must people be to take jobs that fill their pockets yet drain their spirits for the bulk of their waking hours? Why is it so bad?*

These stats were sobering. Surely, people want their lives to matter and make a difference, yet the workplace is failing to fulfill people's needs beyond a paycheck and benefits. Perhaps employees are partially culpable because they're failing themselves by staying in unsatisfying work. It's a mutually damaging downward spiral.

Nearly every CEO I know wants to treat people with respect and dignity—to provide a positive workplace. The pressures upon them to make money are also enormous. Expediency can readily overwhelm engagement.

There just has to be a better way.

Then it hit me. This was the very point Bob was making all along. Gallup provided the evidence of the proverbial elephant dung in the room. The workers and the executives equally suffer from an inherent flaw in the accepted CEO-system. There was this cult-like adherence to the "rules of business" which both sides feared violating.

I said to Bob, "The rules of business are wrong! And, if the rules of business are wrong, then what needs to be rewritten?"

Bob pressed me, "You're incompletely right, but at least now you're asking the right question. Let's not throw the baby out with the bathwater. Based on our discussions where is the misjudgment?"

"We're working at cross-purposes and on personal agendas rather than a unified approach and trust has been broken."

"Yes. When our children were young and bickering with one another, my wife," Bob said, "used a wonderfully apt comparison. She would say, 'Children, you're having a stupid contest. And you're both winning!'"

Lifting his head from looking at his phone to laugh, Chris says, "There's the truth. By the way, I just verified the Gallup stats." Shaking his head in wonder, "What an indictment of business. Okay, you've got my attention and a 147% increase in revenues helps. Those are real dollars. So how do we have no more stupid contests? By the way," Chris the fact-checker asks the CLO, "Where does your company rank on employee engagement?"

Using air quotes, the CLO replies, "We use Gallup to assess our 'Employee' and Customer Engagement. We benchmark against peer companies in the top 80% on both metrics. We're consistently improving."

"Why the air quotes? What's the catch?"

"We don't use the word employee, except when required by government forms. Since Gallup uses employee, we use air quotes around 'employee' to indicate we're using someone else's term."

"What do you call your 'employees,' then?" you ask with an appropriate use of air quotes for effect.

"Team members."

"Why?"

"Because *employee* sets up the traditional employee–employer separation found in CEO-run businesses. Rather than define our relationships within the company by positioning, pay grade, or some other hierarchal 'us–them' construct, we look at competencies and results relative to the work at hand. Team members is a more fluid and autonomous dynamic to organize people around the work to be done and our collective results."

Chris says, "Interesting. So you work really hard to get the right people in the right seats on the bus?"

Chuckling, the CLO says, "Hardly! You're stepping in it today. CLOs avoid that bus analogy. Think about a bus. Passengers get on it, take their seats, and sit behind a bus driver who takes them where he or she decides. That kind of passive and driven analogy accurately depicts CEOs, but it is all wrong in the CLO-system.

"Try this instead," offers the CLO. "Put the right crew in the right roles on the schooner. Or put the right players in the right positions on the team. Both are more fluid and dynamic environments than parking one's rear end in a seat."

Chris smiles in appreciation, "Yep, better. Every person has an important role in helping the ship safely, effectively, and efficiently to its destination. I can see where those examples exemplify team engagement."

The CLO's eyes twinkle as he adds, "Plus it is called leader-*ship*, not leader-*bus*."

After the collective groans subside, Chris says, "Statements like that deserve a mutiny, but I'm going to sail past that comment for now." More groans.

Chris asks, "So how do I put employee engagement in place? What company policy do I need to ensure engagement?"

Chris's question is yet again incredibly typical of CEO-style thinking. Nevertheless, the CLO respectfully answers the question, "Company purpose, not policy, is the origin for 'employee' and customer engagement. There needs to be mutual attraction, alignment, and respect to create the conditions for authentic engagement."

Chris surmises, "So you're talking corporate culture?"

"Yes, but culture is an effect, not the cause." The CLO asks, "Where does corporate culture originate?"

"Duh! With the purpose of the organization," echoes Chris, "since you just told me that."

"Chris, you're a fast study," jokes the CLO. "Purpose starts with the top leader who convenes the team to discern and write the core strategic statements of the organization: its statements of purpose, vision, missions, and values. Remember that the first charge of a CLO is to position the business to be a leader in its chosen field. Engagement begins with crystal clear strategic intent and articulation of this deep strategy. Purpose is then woven into the strategies, tactics, structures, systems, and measures to create conditions for more predictable engagement. We call that being an on-purpose business."

The On-Purpose Principle

The CLO continues, "The Chief Leadership Officer initiates and advances the company conversation. Aligning the purpose of the person with the purpose of the organization creates deep constancy. When what we say about ourselves in our marketing and sales matches our delivered products and services, then we are in integrity.

"Complaints become welcomed feedback because they're clues to where our effectiveness, efficiency, and/or engagement may need to improve. This corporate candor lowers the 'risk-to-do-business-with-us' factor as both a team member and a customer.

"Such trustworthiness produces raving fan customers in online reviews, word-of-mouth introductions, and social media shares. This lower cost of new customer acquisition allows us to invest more in product development, customer research, systems improvement, relationship building, and so forth. The better attuned we are to our customers' needs, the better our products, services, and support become.

"Instead of the business spinning its wheels or worse, spiraling downward fighting within itself and at odds with its customers, we gain traction and then positive forward momentum. Because we've set out to be increasing wealth from the start, our end product is increasing wealth.

"Contrast this with the empty toil of the disengaged 87% whose hearts are not in their work. Every day is at the bidding of someone else's dream and a sell out of their own. Chasing a dollar is an extrinsic motivation that can carry a business or a person only so far. Making lots of money often leaves a person bemoaning, 'There must be more to life than this.'

"Whether the disengaged are victims or self-victimized isn't the question. The greater questions are *Why does the two-*

sided nature of victimization even enter into conversation? Why is there a divided house when there's a greater common cause to serve and achieve as a team?

"'Employee' engagement starts with a leader who sees people as leaders in various stages of competency and is seeking to inspire and instill purpose in their lives and work. In other words: are people assets or human beings? CLOs see people with aspirations and hopes who long to make a contribution that makes the world a better place.

"Given the option of being wholeheartedly engaged in one's work, why not? Why bother just doing a job when we can be answering a call and giving greater expression to our purpose? Who wouldn't want that?"

Chris says, "Great inspirational speech, my friend. You make CEOs out to be some sort of soul devouring ogres. We're not; we're people too with our own set of pressures and imperfections who battle to stay in business, preserve jobs, satisfy investors, and build a life for ourselves and our families too."

The CLO says, "Agreed, but what's your point Chris? Aren't you really making Bob's case that employer and employee alike are locked in 'a stupid contest and both sides are winning'? It isn't that some *thing* has to change. It is that some *one* has to grow."

"Hmmm," murmurs Chris, "I guess you're right. So what do I actually do differently to break the cycle of stupidity?"

Chris begins answering his own question with a deadpan mimic. "Oh yeah. I have to shift my perspective. I have to see people as people—leaders in development. Whew! There's a lot to being a CLO," complained Chris.

"Let's simplify it," says the CLO. "Take off the pretenses, put the mechanics aside, and live the Golden Rule."

"What's the Golden Rule?"

"The Golden Rule says, 'Do to others what you want them to do to you.' Get your heart in the right place and the rest of life and business will more readily fall in place. That's one of the advantages of being in business more completely right.

"Before leaving Latte Out Loud, you'll have a solid understanding of full Engagement to go along with Efficiency and Effectiveness. All that knowledge, however, without a change of heart is just more management, not leadership. Only you can make the choice which you will be."

"Whew!" chirps a more receptive Chris. "Sounds like a plan to me. So what did Bob and you talk about next?"

"Stakeholder Engagement, the people who have a vested interest in your business either formally or by choice."

Chapter 8
Stakeholder Engagement

I enjoy jazz, and one way to think about leadership is
to consider a jazz band. Jazz-band leaders choose music,
find the right musicians, and perform—in public. But the
effect of the performance depends on so many things—the
environment, the volunteers playing in the band, the need for
everyone to perform as individuals and as a group, the
absolute dependence of the leader on the members of the band,
the need of the leader for the followers to play well.
What a summary of an organization!

Max DePree
Former Chairman and CEO, Herman Miller, Inc.
Leadership Jazz
1992

CLG

"We've focused primarily on Team Engagement, the internal aspects of engagement," informed Bob. "Let's shift to Stakeholder Engagement, the interested people outside the organization."

"You mean our customers and shareholders," I said.

"They're part of the stakeholder audience. They are your known, direct touches—customers (clients, guests, patients, patrons, etc.)."

"Bob, you used the words 'direct touches,' the implication being ... what?"

"'Direct touches' are people we've identified and know how to reach them via their contact information. Some of those are active and inactive customers, some are prospective customers. Think about your company address book; it likely includes shareholders, government officials, social media followers, friends, competitors, vendors, peers, journalists, industry bloggers, watchdogs, neighbors, and more."

Bob said, "Consider how LinkedIn is set up to show you your first, second, and third level connections. The Six Degrees of Separation Theory first proposed in 1929 by writer Frigyes Karinthy in a short story called 'Chains' is half visible on LinkedIn—the premise of the theory being that anyone on the planet is only six introductions away from meeting anyone else on the planet.

"The premise speaks to what some call the 'small world' phenomenon. Social media such as LinkedIn, Twitter, Instagram, and Facebook have made us far more connected, accessible, and in communication."

"Bob, with all due respect, social media isn't new."

"True, but consider the implications to a business built on an Industrial Age platform. Traditionally, executives focused on shareholder returns and customer satisfaction as their key, almost exclusive, metrics. Six degrees of separation was impractical. Today, in mere seconds, the President of the United States can tweet or post to tens of millions of followers around the world. Followers can tweet back and retweet to their followers expanding the exposure to hundreds of millions, if not billions of people.

"This degree of direct reach works for and against us. Plus there are independent watchdogs who can influence the value of our reputation, brand, and loyalty. Never before has there been such high outside accountability beyond the Board of Directors.

"Burying our executive heads in the sand about this social accountability and stakeholders is pure folly. Our businesses have worldwide ripple effects and influence. Whereas CEOs largely focus on shareholder returns, CLOs also cultivate stakeholder engagement in order to produce a favorable strategic business vibe as part of positioning the business to be a leader in its chosen field."

Scratching my head in wonderment, I asked, "Where do we start with Shareholder Engagement?"

Bob smiled, "It's Business 101. First do right by your team so they'll do right by your immediate customers by helping them do right by their direct customers and so forth. This is your 'Customer Chain.' Understanding these relationships strategically focuses your process and performance energy and alignment to better serve the Customer Chain.

"FYI, a 3-link customer chain is described as your customers' customers' customers. Depending upon the size of the company, there can be many more links in the Customer Chain.

I joked, "Bob, what are you spluttering about customers? Help me out. What I know is that Marketing 101 says to pick a target audience and serve it. I like the simplicity of that. Seems like you're complicating things."

"In these digital days, that's burying your head in the sand and denying the reality of this highly connected world. Ignoring reality is when business gets complicated. You're actually holding an amazing opportunity to reach and build relationships with valuable niches of customers and stakeholders."

"I get that, but explain how the Customer Chain plays into that."

Bob obliged, "Let's start with my 'spluttering.' The breakdown of the 'customers' customers' customers' goes like this. Your direct customer is known as your (C1) customer. Your customer has their customers who are designated as (C2). And (C2) customers have customers (C3) and so forth (C4 ...).

"Traditional marketing says to address your C1 customers' needs. What better way, however, to serve your C1s' needs than to understand who, why, and how they are serving their customers? This empathic approach informs the marketing and positions the C1 customer to engage with and trust your business because you understand their customers."

"That makes sense, Bob. In essence, we're partnering with our C1 customers to solve their C2 customers' needs and so forth. So this radiates to the C2 and the C3."

Bob confirmed, "In an ocean of possible stakeholders, you have to decide where to drop anchor and fish. Base that decision on your self-interest so you're free to serve in your customers' self-interest.

"The Customer Chain factors in a more complete view of stakeholders beyond the surface of target audiences alone. This deeper view of the influence and contribution of your business improves your marketing penetration and enriches team engagement. Customer stories from C1, C2, C3, and beyond give team members a greater appreciation for how their work is influencing the planet.

"Our actions have always had consequences well beyond our direct customer relationships. Compared to the Industrial Age, our worldwide reach and audience in the Digital Age is more fluidly connected and aware. Even small local businesses can think globally while acting locally."

Shoot for the Moon

Bob asked, "You've likely heard your Pops talk about 'being on the first moon landing' with Apollo 11, right?"

"Absolutely. He still talks about the pride his team and he felt as they listened to the first lunar landing on July 20, 1969. Apparently, several lightweight specialty parts cast in the foundry were used in the fabrication of the Eagle, the lunar module used by Neil Armstrong and Buzz Aldrin to reach and live on the surface of the moon."

Bob informed, "Look at it in terms of the Customer Chain at work."

"That's interesting." Pops told me, "NASA hired Grumman Corporation to design and build the lunar module. Then a Grumman subcontractor hired our foundry to cast the parts."

Bob explained, "That's the start of your Pops' Customer Chain. His customer was the subcontractor, C1. Grumman was C2. NASA was C3. The astronauts were C4. The American people were C5. And the rest of the people in the world were C6. Given the space race, the Russians were especially 'stakeholders' in the outcome, albeit hoping for failure. Success translated into the United States sending a peaceful message to the Russians about the country's fortitude, will, and technological capabilities."

"Click, I get it! Bob, the Customer Chain is the track for focusing and bringing Stakeholder Engagement to life."

Bob said, "Find your version of putting a man on the moon and returning him safely. CLOs start and sustain a company-wide conversation about increasing wealth plus the reach, responsibility, and opportunity the team has to contribute to the common good while caring for one another. All we're doing is aligning self-interested parties along a line of meaning and performance that goes far beyond the financial profit motive."

I respectfully posed, "But Bob, cause marketing has been around for a long time. What's new and different?"

Bob smiled, "Authenticity is what's different. Thanks for that question. We used to *do* cause marketing. It was a do-good, dutiful citizenship supplement. We looked good, felt good, and did good. Not to diminish our sincerity, but it was mostly a public relations and team building exercise.

"We no longer do cause marketing because we are the cause. It isn't duty, it's who we are, what we naturally choose to be engaged in and with. No more add-on afterthought for the sake of appearances.

"The cleansing of a corporate body, mind, and spirit sparks the heart, inspires the mind, and calls us into action. And, I'll add, it seems like one helluva of risk, but it is even riskier being a poser and pleaser."

Surprised by this last comment, I asked, "What makes it so risky?"

"Leading a CLO business runs counter to the old, familiar CEO-system. Change tends to spur resistance. Becoming more completely right rattles many people's point of view.

"When I embarked on our CLO conversion, some longtime team members left on their own accord. They thought I had lost my mind. Even after training and individual coaching, some members no longer fit or wouldn't adjust. Each was given an appropriate placement package. Some pain is an unavoidable part of the growth process."

"But you persevered. Why?"

Bob said, "Once I realized what was at stake, to be so incompletely right was too disadvantaged. I was ready to lead a more fully engaged team. We couldn't move forward clinging to old ways and attitudes.

"Stakeholder Engagement depends upon Team Engagement. To have Team Engagement we needed a high buy-in for who we are and what we value. To reform and lead the business, we needed to be self-led teams with a sincere passion for serving. Our 'house' needed to be right before we invited others in."

Chris observes, "Wow! In so many words, Bob cleaned house."

The CLO says, "Actually, the house mostly cleaned itself. Even so, you can see that Bob was strategic and kind to the people who opted out or were placed out of the company.

"Think about it: former team members are alumni stakeholders, too. How they're treated rests on the Golden Rule, too. Part of the transition from CEO to CLO is taking a stand for the corporate culture and business brand. Junking 'human resources' into a recycling bin is antithetical to the CLO leader.

"By definition, therefore, a top performing company of leaders requires engaged team members who are leaders or developing as leaders. Disengaged people who don't leave a company need to have their futures freed up so they can find a fit where they can engage. Despite the pain, everyone profits when that happens."

Chris says, "I've a few people whose 'futures need to be freed up.'"

"Chris," asks the CLO, "might you still be in management mode?"

"Huh?" asks Chris.

"If a person is disengaged in the company, who is to blame? Who hired the person? Who trained them? Who coached and led them?"

Chris sheepishly says, "Ultimately I did. I set up the systems, or didn't, to assess fit and equip them to succeed. So I'm the responsible party?"

"You're culpable for the system. Within the system, however, each person is responsible for leading their lives and work. For CLOs, we wisely invest in people when we first engage their services, and even when they leave us. Every departure from the business is a mutual learning and improvement experience for all of us. If the person is open to it, why not take advantage of the lessons?"

An impatient Chris says, "Fast forward this story to the results. You risked becoming a CLO, so how's business?"

The CLO answers, "Thriving. Doing so much good for so many stakeholders is such a better, more complete way of doing business. Naturally, a more complete business is more likely to produce better business results across all measures."

Chris inquires, "So it's like the cafe owners here and their business? They're well aware of Stakeholder Engagement."

"I would agree," says the CLO. "That's probably why

Latte Out Loud was recommended to me this morning. It was probably one of their Stakeholders."

As if toasting with his coffee mug, Chris lifts it high in the air and revels, "There's so much more here than a single great cup of coffee. I'm drinking in their story—the way they designed and built their business around what matters most to them. It's about how they're involving others to further engage in their vision and missions.

"Before today, I didn't even know coffee grew in Ethiopia. Now I'm inexplicably rooting for their success. I'll like and follow their social media to get updates on their local involvement and planned trip. Hey, I've become a non-financial investor!"

The CLO kids, "You need to become a financial investor. Remember, you're paying for the coffee."

Chris feigns a protest, "Hey, what gives? Do you normally stick your driver with the bill?" Dramatically reaching into his pants pocket Chris unfurled his choking wad of folded over Benjamin Franklins and says, "Ha! So be it, cheapskate. No problem. I can afford it." Peeling off a $100 bill, Chris dramatically slaps it on the table indicating he's covering the check.

Even comedic arrogance is still arrogant. Chris's theatric overcompensation is part of his charm—and not. Ordinarily, he wouldn't behave like that, but he trusted us as friends to take his joke as intended.

Exchanging glances with the CLO and then mutual head nods you non-verbally agree that Chris's payment is acceptable restitution for such boorish behavior.

"A-greed," utters the CLO.

"That settles that," Chris comments.

Capitalism Is Caring
Chris continues, "From a pure business perspective, how profitable can this coffee shop be? In their own earthy and

charitable way, they're obviously working hard to make a go of it. What motivates them to work so hard?"

The CLO agrees, "That x-factor comes from being in business on-purpose. There's an animated vibe and spirited authenticity where even the mundane tasks hold meaning and contribution. That's high engagement—the capacity to look beyond the matter at hand and envision how it fits into the larger vision."

Chris is in analysis mode, "But I have to wonder if doing business this way is scalable beyond one cafe?"

The CLO asks, "Have you heard of Whole Foods Market, Great Harvest Bread Company, Ben & Jerry's Ice Cream, Patagonia clothes, method soap, or Tom's Shoes? They've scaled nicely."

"Point made," concedes Chris. "I've not heard of all those companies, but of the ones I know, they've definitely scaled and model many of the qualities you're describing. I've read about these kinds of businesses that seek to be social capitalists. Seems like an oxymoron but they make it work by combining a social mission as a part of their core strategy."

"'Social capitalists' aren't new. It's just business people are finally returning companies to their true calling," informs the CLO. "Business was always intended to improve humanity. We business people perverted it from collaboratively increasing wealth to competitively enriching ourselves often at the expense of others. Win–lose is a bad long-term business recipe."

Chris closes his eyes as if using a mental browser, "I keep up with corporate law. There's a relatively new type of corporation called a Benefits Corporation or B-Corp. The stated ends of their corporate charters are a hybrid of a for-profit corporation and a not-for-profit organization. They too speak in terms of stakeholders and not just shareholders. B-Corps institutionalize what we've been talking about. That's more evidence that this CLO thing is plausible."

The CLO shares, "A business reformation is underway and B-Corps, for example, are one of the signs. Recovering from the downside effects of the Industrial Age, the re-humanization of being in business and doing good sets the stage for unparalleled opportunities and profit."

Chris confesses, "I am rethinking things. Previously I threw B-Corps into the category of being corporate hipsters. It's kinda like a few got lucky and broke it big. They garnered attention for being socially responsible and traditionally profitable, but I saw them as economic sideshows. If you're right, they may actually emerge as the main show."

"Agreed," says the CLO.

Chris says, "On paper, if I were the owner of this building, I'm not sure I would have leased this space to Nala and her husband for Latte Out Loud. I would have assessed this coffee shop idea as flaky and wishful thinking—too high a risk for eventual eviction. I would expect to come by here in a month or two and see a vacant sign in the front door. Today, all other things being equal, they've strategically improved their probability for success because they've kept it simple. This inviting place has a great cup of coffee and a loyal following. The owners are sincere, authentic, and likable."

Chris pauses, twists his face, and slowly says, "I kinda get it ... and I kinda don't. Just how do businesses like this stay in business?"

The CLO laughs, "Bob Scott lifted me over this same quandary by helping me appreciate pure goodwill."

Chris's ears perk up, "You mean goodwill, as in commercial goodwill? That unrealistic 'premium,'" Chris made air quotes, "that every business owner selling a business uses to jack up the sale price of the business over the asset value?"

The CLO says, "Yes, that one. Keep listening, you might learn something."

Chapter 9
Fluidity

I have found it helpful to keep constantly in mind
that there are really two entries to be made
for every transaction—
one in terms of immediate dollars and cents,
the other in terms of goodwill.

Ralph Hitz
Austrian Hotel Pioneer
1891–1940

CLO

I asked Bob, "Do CLOs have disdain for the financial metrics?"

"Hardly," he answered. "CLOs hold a more complete view of business. The numbers reveal just one part of the company's state of being. We're akin to doctors with a good bedside manner who focus on the person and not just the patient's vital statistics. This holistic approach is the better way to build a healthier business.

"Because numbers are so deceptively tangible and seemingly accurate, managing primarily by the financial statements is alluring. Ultimately, however, it is the story behind the numbers that reveals how best to lead a team.

"There's a dynamic tension always at work between revenues and relationship. Many business people, especially CEOs, 'resolve' this tension by being financially fixated. This self-defeating and incomplete approach inflicts misdirected pressure on the team and underperformance by the business. Yet it seems to be the preferred pattern of many a CEO. But, then again, most of those CEOs don't end up sitting in my office. It is easy for them to pound for profits in some self-deceived belief that they're doing a great job."

I pressed, "Okay, but in practical terms, how does 'a good bedside manner' translate into business performance?"

"In two words: pure goodwill," Bob answered. "Pure goodwill is the organizational weal and value which is largely attributed to the reputation, relationships, and fluidity of the company."

"Fluidity? What's that?"

"Fluidity is how smoothly a business performs as a complete system. A highly fluid business flows effortlessly primarily because it is so well designed, integrated, and productive. Financial profit is the natural by-product of the business fulfilling its purpose with fluidity."

Jokingly, I asked, "And if a company lacks fluidity, what's that called?"

"Stopped up or constricted. Blockages, friction, and/or fragmentation in the system slow it down. Such organizational dis-integration causes complexity and difficulty for team members and customers alike."

"I relate to the constricted part all too well. I didn't realize it before, but I want fluidity for the business."

Bob said, "And today, you'll gain that understanding of how CLOs get a business flowing."

As an aside Bob added, "On a personal note, Hal Trudy, my mentor and a younger business colleague of your Pops, opened my eyes to the risks of being financially nearsighted. What a joy it must be for your Pops to see his legacy come to life in a great-grandchild. I'm so honored to be a part of this succession from your Pops to Hal to me and now you."

I said, "Me too." I still wasn't sold that this CLO thing was for real or for me. Nevertheless, Bob and I chatted briefly about Pops and some of the lessons Hal passed on to him.

Intangible Results

"So how does goodwill play into being a CLO?"

Pointing out his window to a park across the street, Bob said, "See that bench nestled among those flowers with the large overhanging oak tree? That's where Hal Trudy and I periodically sit and talk business. He calls that bench his 'branch office' because of the large limb protecting it. One day, Hal and I were reviewing my financial statements when he pointed out a line item called, 'Goodwill' and asked me if I knew what it meant."

I replied to Hal, "Goodwill is a number on the balance sheet to account for and recognize the value of intangible assets such as patents, licenses, brand equity, trademarks, and proprietary technology. Compared to tangible assets like equipment, buildings, and machinery with ready markets, putting a final value on these assets is difficult to assess until a time of sale or transfer. I think of goodwill as the premium (or discount) a buyer willingly pays for the business. With so many variables, goodwill is a soft number because it is hard to quantify."

Hal said, "True, some intangible assets can be sold apart from the going concern. This means they can be appraised using the replacement cost, income, and market value methods.

"There's also a class of intangible assets that is indivisible from the business. My CLO colleagues and I refer to them as 'pure goodwill.' Every company has pure goodwill by default or by design. It's inseparable from the business because it is the strategic and performance value of the company's fluidity based on the strength of reputation, stories, experiences, relationships, and systems independent of any specific person or persons. Pure goodwill is the degree of trust and integrity of the corporate person—its spirit and personality that can be low or high. Investment bankers translate it in terms of a 'multiple' relative to similarly indexed companies."

Hal asked, "Are you catching the implications?"

Answering him, I said, "Pure goodwill is news to me. What a riddle! Basically, you're telling me that there's this unrecognized, off-balance-sheet value that's an even more subjective measure than the divisible intangibles assets."

"Precisely, and imprecisely, too," joked Hal. "The difference between managers and leaders is their focus. Managers administer the tangible assets and liabilities seeking to produce financial profit. They're doing business incompletely right.

"Leaders, on the other hand, integrate the entirety of the business—tangible and intangible assets, and liabilities—to profit everyone. Pure goodwill is ultimately the measure of the CLO's integrative leadership and management capability and performance."

"Bob's sharing of Hal's statements stopped me cold," admits the CLO. "None of this even beeped on my CEO radar. I was blind to pure goodwill and fluidity! I never saw it as indicative of my leadership.

"No wonder our operations and ethics coexisted in parallel instead of being a unified enterprise. As the leader, it was my job to improve business fluidity. I mouthed our purpose and values but had no systemic way for us to walk our talk. Nor did I have a way to measure pure goodwill.

"Numbers, buildings, and machinery don't grow our business. Purpose, plans, people, processes, and performance to customers do. When these are smoothly aligned, then our corporate culture is setting us apart and gives a unique strategic advantage and value in the marketplace. Beyond our business model, it's our service model that defines us and creates a premium value for our customers."

Shooting forward in his chair, Chris proclaims, "Guilty! Just like Bob and you! Pure goodwill? Fluidity? Never heard of them. Never really factored them into my business thinking."

The CLO says, "Chris, in truth you're unconsciously factoring them into your thinking. Now that you have the pure goodwill and fluidity terminology you'll be more aware."

"And I can measure and value them," Chris adds.

"Yes, you've looked into the white space that supports the tangible, gives it completeness, and plays an essential part of the overall business design."

"'White space?' What's that?"

The CLO offers an example, "When you read a book, you see black words printed on a white page. The white space is the blank page that holds, frames, and contrasts with the printed words and images. Because the white space falls into the background most readers don't give it a second thought. Yet the white space is hard at work as an essential part of the overall design of the reading experience.

"Leaders are like graphic layout artists. We work the entire page and contents. Solid leaders, like effective design, set up the business design and systems to highlight the content of the work being performed by the company. A leader's job that's well done tends to fade into the background.

"Out of necessity, entrepreneurs typically develop an instinct for the white space. In the start-up they have to design and develop the intangible and the tangible—the white space and the print. This causes them to see the business more completely. In time, this entrepreneurial experience, perspective, and instinct can become a source of mutual frustration between managers and founders.

"Managers tend to only see the print on the page. This is why a leader and a manager can look at the same page and draw very different conclusions."

"Whew, do I relate to that! Now that you point out the white space of the business, I see that it's always been there. I've never focused on it as part of the more complete picture.

"How do I measure an intangible?" Chris asks.

The CLO explains. "Every thing can be measured. Some things are easier than others. Corporate culture and engagement surveys, for instance, can be a part of a CLO's scorecard along with the normal business metrics. Without them, we get a skewed view of the increasing wealth performance.

"Industrial Age thinking dumbed down pure goodwill to be just the financial premium or discount over book value that an acquiring company pays the selling company. From a legal and accounting standard this post-sale valuation is correct treatment. Building pure goodwill is a CLO's focus in the normal course of being in business."

Chris closes his eyes and gently shakes his head in thought as he speaks, "I get it, but I don't. An example would help."

"Sure. Minutes ago," the CLO reminds, "the three of us experienced an increase in pure goodwill. When Nala, our barista, shared about her husband's and her Ethiopian coffee growers and local community missions, her enthusiasm planted a seed in us that evoked greater customer interest and loyalty. We're more favorably inclined to frequent Latte Out Loud and to spread their story via word-of-mouth and social media. This goodwill shows up indirectly in potentially higher sales and a lower cost of marketing that creates higher profits with no additional financial investment in equipment, marketing, facilities, and such."

"I get it," says Chris. "Good service and kindness pay! There's no doubt that pure goodwill is real and is eventually realized when a business is sold. I guess the point is that the economics of an ethos is typically out of sight and out of mind. And this oversight comes with a price regardless of whether we measure it or not."

"Nailed it, Chris!" praises the CLO. To which the ever effusive Chris raised clenched fists high in the air as a sign of personal victory and lets out a loud, "Yes!"

The Top Line on The Bottom Lines

Suddenly a zealot, Chris points to the CLO and demands, "What are CLOs doing to be leading more completely right in order to improve fluidity and increase pure goodwill?"

"One way," the CLO explains, "is the development and use of a double or triple bottom line. In 1994, John Elkington, the founder of SustainAbility, proposed three bottom lines for businesses.

1. The Financial Account: the traditional measures of corporate profit
2. The People Account: social responsibility through operations
3. The Planet Account: environmental responsibility

"Elkington's triple bottom line illustrates what's possible. Social and environmental responsibility reflect his interests. CLOs modify Elkington's model to suit their unique interests.

"CLOs have three bottom lines: Financial, People, and Purpose. This triple-bottom-line view is a more comprehensive assessment for increasing wealth."

Inhaling this fresh knowledge, Chris inquires, "What goes in the Purpose account?"

The CLO thinks, "It depends on a company's preferences and priorities. Nala and her husband invest locally and in Ethiopia. Our now favorite coffee shop owners might replace Elkington's 'environmental responsibility' with 'economic development.'"

Chris says, "That makes sense that each company defines these extra bottom lines for itself. What's the CLO's role in all of this?"

"As always, we're positioning the business to be a leader in its chosen field. As the pivotal corporate officer we're engaging our board and team to define and align the three bottom lines."

Chris admits, "Have I been negligent to the business and team?"

Commiserating, the CLO says, "Once I understood the impact of what was possible through my leadership position and the incompletely right nature of my traditional CEO job description, I felt the same way. Bob suggested I use the Chief Leadership Officer title as the more complete description of my higher stewardship. It's an audible, visual, and practical departure from the CEO-run system for my benefit. Every time I use CLO it reminds me what sets me apart from being a CEO.

"This more robust CLO understanding and level of accountability is exhilarating and fun. As a company, we're being in business the way it was intended. We're all working toward high fluidity. Beyond pure goodwill is pure joy! That's what we're all working to achieve."

"Seems like a bunch of work to get there," notes Chris.

"Sure, but we were doing a bunch of work before anyway, especially because we had so much friction. So the work is the easy part. It is the retraining of our brains and manners that has been on the learning curve.

"It has required personal growth and maturity of leadership to guide the business from a CEO-run to a CLO-led business, but I have no regrets. Instinctively, I just knew there had to be a better way to be in business. I accepted Bob's proposed CLO title at the time as being an aspirational reminder that I was free from the limitations of doing business as just a CEO."

Chris looks at you and sarcastically says, "Okay, that's it! Got my answer. Now I know why he calls himself a CLO. We're done here."

You look askance at him as if to say *Really, Chris?*

Chris winks and retorts, "I was testing to see if you were still paying attention. That's why I got you coffee. I just knew this conversation would be so-o boring and irrelevant. Always is with this guy," as he casually flipped a hand in the direction of the CLO.

The CLO dismisses Chris's ribbing with a couple of

disbelieving shakes of his head sideways. Yet again choosing to ignore Chris's antics, he shifts in his seat, slightly turns his back to Chris, and asks you, "So, are you wondering what happened next with Bob Scott?"

Chris butts in, "Sure, I'm very interested. This CLO thing is still a mystery but I'm on the case now."

Squaring off to the table, the CLO graces Chris's comment with, "I'm so glad you are. Let's break this case open."

"Go for it," Chris encourages, "What did Bob tell you next?"

Chapter 10
Unfinished Business

"Your first role . . . is the personal one. It is the relationship
with people, the development of mutual confidence, the
identification of people, and the creation of a community.
This is something only you can do. It cannot be measured or
easily defined. But it is not only a key function. It is one only
you can perform."

Peter Drucker
Management Consultant, Educator, and Author
In a letter written to Bob Buford
1909–2005

CLO

Reflecting on his past Bob Scott said, "Once I recognized
how incompletely right I was 'leading' the company, I was
compelled to do and be in business differently. I needed to step
up my game as a leader."

In this moment of remembrance, for the first time, Bob's
body language was heavy. I asked him, "You sound like you
were genuinely distressed. What happened at your park bench
conversations with Hal?"

"Hal opened my eyes to the errors of my blunt force
business approach and other omissions such as neglecting our
pure goodwill and fluidity. I had a bottom line philosophy:
make more money. Everyone and everything was bent to my
will. No one doubted who owned MY business. My name
was on the door and everyone knew it; and I mean everyone
—customers, employees, and vendors. It was all about me.

"With every manager and employee, I beat a drum of
'profit, profit, profit.' To me, it was simple: get on board to

grow sales, reduce costs, invest in productivity, and make more money. Candidly, customers were numbers—transactions needed to serve my business agenda and personal financial goals. Every contract was an arms-length, win–lose battle ultimately won or lost over price. Every day in the office was a P&L siege in the marketplace. Every employee was on a pure ROI measure. Produce, save, or leave."

I related to his situation. We were in different businesses, but the states of our business minds were remarkably alike. "Bob, you're describing my daily grind."

He pressed on, "Exhausting, isn't it?"

"You bet."

Continuing his story, he said, "As the CEO I was an inflicting manager instead of an inspiring leader. But I didn't have a clue how to right it so I insanely did what I always did. I talked louder, faster, and more frequently about making our numbers. I worked longer hours and expected the same from my employees. I set numerical goals and expected people to figure out how to get there."

"Hal's the first person I respected enough who intervened, caught my attention, and pointed out my folly. He introduced me to the three charges of a Chief Leadership Officer about positioning and integrating for leadership.

"They seemed simple enough, but I fought them. I was stuck in my ways. As far as what Hal and your Pops were proposing to me—moving from a traditional CEO-run system of business to a CLO-led approach—it appeared to be far too radical of a restructuring for my comfort. My plate was full so I dug in my heels and resisted them.

"They encouraged me to become a CLO pioneer, to help explore and map uncharted territory. At the time, I was proud of my 'fully functioning, profitable' enterprise; and I subscribed to the old adage, *If it ain't broke, don't fix it*. The business was sufficiently successful to sustain a comfortable lifestyle for my family and me. I paid my employees fair wages where they could do the same. What was so bad about that exchange?"

I asked, "Bob, in those days did you sense something was wrong in your business?"

"Yes. Like my peers, I built an organization that sufficiently produced a product and an income stream. I created jobs that bought people's time but didn't engage their hearts and minds. I never set out to build an 'Increasing Wealth' business, so we operated in a profitable, yet disengaging range below our potential. I didn't realize how much of an unfinished business I had."

"An unfinished business," echoes Chris. "You CLOs have a gracious way of expressing it."

"Gracious, perhaps," says the CLO, "but I prefer to see it as an accurate depiction of the normal state of a CEO-run business. There's an incompleteness to the design and build-out, an inherent blind spot or structural defect preventing the business from more fully expressing its purpose as well as its profit-making potential."

Chris asks, "Is this where your term 'incompletely right' originated?"

"Yes. CEO-run organizations are in a constant improvement process in the areas of moneymaking and business management, but they're running on only one of three cylinders. It sounds good, but it ignores the inherent promise of business to be increasing wealth so everyone profits. Perhaps this explains why the media portrays business persons as shallow, greedy, self-serving people who only care about themselves.

"When, in fact, business people are generally some of the most diligent, risk-tasking, hard-working, responsible servers in society. Our actions open us to being judged as the former, not the latter."

"The disconnect, then," Chris concludes, "is our unfinished business. And everyone pays the price."

"Exactly," says the CLO. "Let me show you what Hal and Bob gave me."

Chapter 11
The CLO Integrity Map

To give real service you must add something
which cannot be bought or measured with money,
and that is sincerity and integrity.

Douglas Adams
Author, *The Hitchhikers Guide to the Galaxy*

Pops would say, "Inspiration without perspiration is a fancy name for wishful thinking." Up to this point, Bob's and my conversations were conceptual about CLO. I needed more grist for the mill, so I asked Bob for something to *do* along with *being* a CLO. "How do I implement being a CLO?"

From his desk, Bob picked up a couple of pieces of paper. Handed one to me and keeping the other, he said, "Here's 'the Chief Leadership Officer (CLO) Integrity Map' or our shorthand for it is, 'the Map.'"

Reviewing the Map, I knew further explanation was

needed. Bob willingly obliged me.

"The Map guides CLOs to design, position, and build their business to become a leader in its chosen field. An income statement and balance sheet reflect financial health. An organizational chart portrays the hierarchal structure of a typical CEO-run company. Similarly, the CLO Integrity Map defines the fundamental relationships, alignment, and flow from organizational purpose into meaningful performance. The Map naturally integrates the intangibles and the tangibles —pure goodwill and organizational purpose—into the business functions through to the customer experience. Finally, we evaluate the effects on the triple bottom lines in order to 'Re-Think' the Map as part of our ongoing constant improvement process."

I posed, "The Map provides an added facet or dimension to view the business more completely?"

"Yes," Bob confirmed. "But it shifts the primary focus of the CLO and team to leading and thinking instead of being slaves to numbers and hierarchy. Instead of the team being so managerially burdened, they are actually freed up to perform their work, assume responsibilities, and make local decisions consistent with the business purpose and plan. Treating people like people instead of mindless objects awakens their worth and invites them to more fully participate in their work as a calling."

Resuming the orientation, Bob said, "Across the top of the CLO Integrity Map are five progressive stages: Articulation> Synthesis> Development> Performance> Re-Think. Below them, the watermark arrow within the Map indicates flow from one stage to the next is left to right, a symbol of relationships, movement, and progress."

Looking it over, I said, "This seems straightforward and, no offense, somewhat simplistic and generic. We already do a lot of this stuff shown in the boxes."

Matter-of-factly, Bob countered. "Probably not, at least in

this order and context. The Map complements Frederick Taylor's world of conformity and standardization by energizing people with purpose and meaning. That's the strategic advantage for companies today and tomorrow.

"For people directly involved in a business, the CLO Integrity Map amplifies team members' meaningful contributions while strengthening their sense of belonging and significance. By authentically integrating humanity and work, we offset the downside effects of Taylor's principles. The pure goodwill effect is to improve the fluidity of the workplace through a variety of often imperceivable gains and savings that collectively improve the workplace and profits.

"Honoring and valuing personhood invites creativity, innovation, and intelligence. In Taylor's world, these qualities were uninvited guests that defied Industrial Age drive for non-variance from standards.

"This Map overviews the key relationships and waypoints that are vital for a CEO to become a CLO, and for the company to follow suit. Within it are sub-models, disciplines, and details that each organization customizes to setting. This is the big picture for CLOs and their teams so they can co-create a CLO Integrity Map Playbook, a more detailed and local guide for positioning the business and people to be mutually integrated leaders."

I observed, "So this is how CLOs position the business to be a leader in its chosen field. The Map finishes the unfinished business?"

Bob acknowledged both of my observations with a simple nod and "Yes."

Continuing my orientation, Bob said, "Each stage on the Map heads an imaginary column holding content boxes within it. Let's dig deeper into each column.

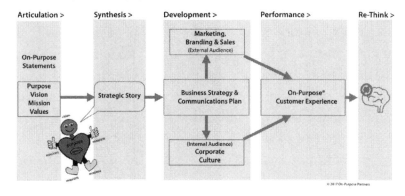

Chief Leadership Officer Integrity Map

© 2017 On-Purpose Partners

"Articulation is the deep strategy, thinking, and writing of the purpose, vision, missions, and values. Collectively, they're called the On-Purpose Statements. By definition and by their presence, these statements are the distinguishing bedrock of a CLO-led organization. The specific meaning, properties, and ordering of Purpose, Vision, Missions, and Values energize the Synthesis, Development, Performance, and Re-Think stages and lend a CLO-led business its unique market characteristics and advantages apart from its tangible assets."

An Inherent Force for the Good

"Of all of them, the purpose statement is the heart and soul of the business. Purpose is organizational DNA—the purest codification and highest power for why the business exists and its call to serve humanity. Purpose is an inherent force for good, never for evil. It allows us to be in our calling rather than being meaninglessly driven in the mindless occupation of making a buck."

I asked, "Personal integrity? Is that another reason it is called the CLO Integrity Map?"

Bob confirmed, "Yes. The On-Purpose Statements are like bottling leadership. Every team member is offered training to write his or her personal set of On-Purpose Statements and develop a career Map.

"Invariably team members begin leading their lives better

which benefits the workplace. People who are clear about who they are, where they're headed, and how to contribute tend to make more informed and better decisions aligned with the company's strategic focus. In short, they're better positioned to more authentically lead on and off the job."

I took note, "The second charge of the CLO—positioning people to be leaders on and off their jobs?"

"Absolutely. The replication on a personal basis primes team members to understand and engage with the organizational purpose and the company-wide use of the Map. By unifying our language and method of leadership, the 3Es of efficiency, effectiveness, and engagement can thrive in unison."

"Bob, what an extraordinary investment in your team! After all, there's only one CLO, yet it seems like you're expecting everyone to be a CLO."

Inching his head back and tilting it slightly to the right I read his body language to indicate mild surprise at my statement. Recovering quickly, he said, "You know I've been a CLO for so long now, that I don't even think of this training and coaching as an investment. It's a necessity to our way of being in business and communicating throughout the company. I shudder to think where we would be without it. Of course, there's only one person with the title CLO, but if everyone is to be a business leader then each person needs to think and act like the CLO. Freeing up people to be the best version of themselves is the only way to be in business, period."

Facts Inform, Stories Transform

Grabbing a pen from his pocket, Bob drew a big circle around the elements of Articulation and Synthesis, thereby taking in the Strategic Story. Pointing with the tip of his pen, Bob said, "Business leaders combine the production, profits, and people into a more complete business.

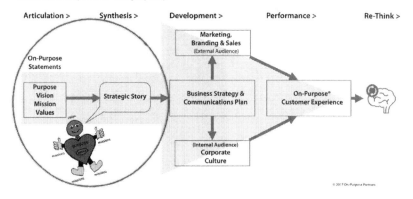

"Purpose is the unifying source that is informing and flowing throughout the length of the CLO Integrity Map, but it needs to be readily grasped by any stakeholder.

"Facts inform and stories transform. Purpose, vision, missions, and values—the words of leadership and strategy— are clinical leadership jargon. Everyone loves a great story that's memorable and worth repeating.

"CLOs employ story-telling techniques to make our strategy applicable and sticky for our various audiences who may not have our clinical curiosity.

"For example, despite our deep strategy On-Purpose and Map training initiatives, some team members have just a passing interest in our company strategy and alignment efforts. That's just the way it is. Stories are highly instructive with those team members at informing and forming our company culture.

"The Strategic Story, therefore, becomes a conversational method and tool that breathes greater life and stickiness to the On-Purpose Statements for use throughout the Map."

People Are Greater Than Process

Tracing the arrow from Synthesis to Development Bob said, "Next is the 'Business Strategy & Communications Plan.' Keeping in mind our internal and external stakeholders— team members and the Customer Chain, respectively—we're simultaneously developing the Business Strategy & Communications Plan with a keen eye for forming connections and fostering engagement.

"As a team that shares common terms and methods for leading, we mitigate a number of communication challenges. Standards conventions are to everyone's advantage."

Placing his pen on the northerly pointing arrow Bob said, "The box reading, 'Marketing, Branding & Sales,' faces our external audience—our Customer Chain." Now following the southernly arrow, he continued, "The Corporate Culture includes the team members and business operation. Together, they are two sides of the same coin that form the On-Purpose Customer Experience. More on this later. Right now, this is just an overview of the Map."

Bob rested his pen on the box reading: On-Purpose Customer Experience. He stated, "We arrived at the Performance column by starting with the purpose of the organization and we infuse it into every stage of the CLO Integrity Map. Having systematically designed the business to be true to who we are—why we exist, what we envision, what we do, and what we value—then we are on our purpose or on-purpose. When the inside, operational, and cultural aspects of the business team and the outside messaging and relationships with customers are consistent, we're in integrity. The product of our purpose and preparation translates into better performance."

I asked, "What happens when your Customer Experience or Performance doesn't meet your standards?"

Re-Think

"Nice segue," thanked Bob. "The last column is Re-Think. We're constantly and intentionally evaluating ourselves along the CLO Integrity Map for pockets of improvement. Re-Think is a term for reviewing, adapting, and refreshing the Map by constantly cycling through it to find grit or friction that hampers our fluidity.

"With everyone on the team trained to use the Map, we identify, classify, and correct isolated problems and system flaws faster, in context, and more precisely. This ongoing team effort to streamline the Map reduces frustration, breaks down traditional departmental silos, and keeps everyone focused on increasing wealth."

I concluded, "And this stimulates organizational integrity?"

Bob said, "Absolutely. And best of all ..." Bob took a long pause.

"What's that?" I asked.

"We have a minimally viable system in place. This means my three charges as a CLO are built and functioning to the point where contextual constant improvement is possible. Because people are free to lead within the company, I'm free to actually be a better leader. With the missing parts of the unfinished business in place, the team and the business are more completely competent and functioning. Leading a company of leaders is beautiful place to be for all of us."

The CLO displays the CLO Integrity Map on his tablet. He visually traces us through the steps of Bob's orientation. Scanning it, Chris says, "I can see why the Map is so powerful and useful for aligning an organization's purpose and infrastructure. I like the flow and logic—but details. I want details."

The CLO promises, "You'll have those."

"Great," says Chris. "Before you share this, something is really bothering me. Bob Scott leads a big business. You now have a mid-market business. What about the smaller business owners? Where do I free the time from doing business to develop a CLO Integrity Map?"

The CLO says, "Oh! Great question. The Map scales to any sized business. As small business owners you have an advantage because you're more agile. In under 30 days, you can be well on your way with all of this."

"Really?" a shocked Chris asks.

"Recall," says the CLO, "that each team member learns how to use and apply the Map to their work. This adaptability readily accommodates the solo owner or small business owner. A start-up entrepreneur can use it to lay out a first pass in an hour. Because 'Re-Think' is the last stage, they will iterate with each revisit adding speed and constant improvement."

Sensing that Chris isn't getting it, the CLO says, "Remember when we were kids learning to play tennis?"

"Sure. That was a lot of years ago."

"You practiced every day to get better. Using the CLO Integrity Map is like that. The more you use and practice with it, the more skilled you'll become. This is not a one and done event. Rather it is an ongoing business lifestyle. Avoid getting hung up on putting it together perfectly from the start. Rather just get started using it as a part of your business leadership and thinking. Like any skill, with time and consistent use, you'll improve over time and eventually gain mastery."

"Uh, but what does it mean to 'use' it?"

"Simple. Now that you've learned the basics, jot down what each stage of the Map looks like to you. Email it to me and we'll walk through a refinement process."

"Okay, then what?"

"Then get your team to work on it with you. Use it in weekly team meetings. Create a scorecard to measure your three bottom lines. The rule of thumb is to check your progress at least as often as you review your numbers but a minimum of weekly. You want this to be the living, vibrant focus in the business, but not a consuming perfection that distracts you from doing the business. Work with it, check it, and rework it.

Increasing Wealth Warning

"Watch out! When you release the leadership potential and talent in your team to think, decide, and be leaders you'll be amazed at how rapidly the CLO Integrity Map comes to life. Over time the team and you will finely tune your CLO Integrity Map."

With a sing-song voice, Chris jokingly adds, "So we can be Increasing Wealth so everyone profits."

Smiling at Chris's mimicry, the CLO shifts into a parental voice, "Yes, Little Chris."

Returning to adult mode the CLO says, "Do you want to hear what Bob shared with me next about Articulation and Synthesis?"

"Yes. I'm all ears," responds Chris.

Chapter 12
The Forgotten Articulation and Synthesis

Money cannot buy peace of mind.
It cannot heal ruptured relationships,
or build meaning into a life that has none.

Richard M. DeVos
Cofounder of Amway Corporation

Bob Scott continued, "The On-Purpose Statements, the On-Purpose Pal, and the Strategic Story, these three elements are highly related and foundational to informing the Development phase: Business Strategy & Communications Plan. From there it branches into the external and internal audiences only to converge to create the On-Purpose Customer Experience.

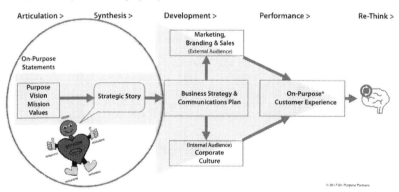

"When what a company promises to deliver through its external messaging is highly correlated to the internal operations and delivery, then integrity is the result. That kind of external and internal consistency is the mark of an On-Purpose Customer Experience.

"The Map move left to right for sustainable systemic improvement. It is as simple as cause and effect.

"Purpose is the source powering the entire CLO system, whereas traditionally, CEOs start at the money problem and work backward. It's expedient but patchy. One idiosyncratic fix begets another, then another, and pretty soon the entire 'system' is compromised. People are breaking into competing tribes with departmental heads, read warlords, fighting one another instead of delivering on the Customer Experience and promise."

"Wow, Bob. Hearing that, I see where we're headed to that place."

Integration or Disintegration

What Bob said next stopped me cold, "Any organization is either in the process of integrating or disintegrating. Leaders understand that decay is naturally occurring. Every organization is always susceptible to falling into a state of disintegration. Countering it takes commitment and work. Forward progress as depicted on the Map is like fighting gravity. CLOs are the resistance fighters whose most fierce battlefronts often begin with the words, "That's the way we do it here." We are the integrators of the whole and purpose is our starting point for integration."

"I never realized that," I admitted to Bob, "but it makes sense."

Bob continued, "Articulation and Synthesis remain the most understated and misunderstood components on the CLO Integrity Map. Traditional CEOs can be quick to discount them as abstract and irrelevant to the 'real work' of the business—making money. Such hollow thinking leads to thin margins."

I had to chuckle, "You're walking a fine line here between

beating up on CEOs and respecting them. What gives with that tough love approach?"

"That's because I empathize with them. I was a CEO who became a CLO. Business is a high and noble calling of service. Yet in the current climate, we've succumbed to crude measures of success.

"Business today resembles the feudal system of the Middle Ages. CEOs are the 'lords.' Some are abusive, some are benevolent, and most are somewhere in between; but it is a type of unspoken caste system. At one time hierarchy and fear may have produced results, but such a dehumanizing combination is too expensive to sustain. And, it is just plain wrong.

"Employers and employees who remain faithful subjects of the archaic ways unwittingly share a collective resignation to mediocrity. It is all they know, they don't believe it can change, or they don't have a replacement. So why try? Don't rock the boat.

"Even though CEOs perpetuate the contemporary feudal system I give my former peers a lot of grace. They're best positioned to change it from within and leave a legacy of leadership. Start-up entrepreneurs can get it right from the start if they'll model the CLO approach.

"Truthfully, we need each another to innovate current practices and usher in a business reformation on a worldwide scale. Such momentum can ultimately eradicate meaningless work while expanding individual opportunities and the economy. That's my crusade, the one your Pops and Hal have passed on to me."

The CLO movement was becoming increasingly significant. All I could say to Bob was, "Wow! Below the surface of my business lives an abiding desire to know my life had meaning and matters for whatever years I have on this big blue orb called Earth. And I want my work to matter."

Bob agreed, "CLOs feel that way and are acting upon it.

CEOs do too but remain mired in the past. Many have in place the talent, influence, resources, and businesses to embrace the CLO-approach, but it is too disturbing to the security of the people who believe they are the disruptors. Taylorism is deeply rooted as the only 'executive' standard. Leadership illiteracy is so widespread that anything different is destructively discounted as being soft."

"Destructive? That's an extreme word," I remarked. "How so?"

Bob detailed, "The CEO model is crazy making. It praises managers and conformity, all the while crushing the very leaders and innovation it longs to have. Too often we ask, 'Where are the leaders?' And yet we're the ones who run them out the door with our mixed messages and lip service to the elements enhancing pure goodwill and fluidity.

"Distrust is bred because the executives are so well organized at being out of integrity with the true purpose of business. Check it yourself. CEOs place their purpose, vision, missions, and values on the walls of their headquarters, print them in annual reports, post them on company websites in the 'About Us' menu. They reference them in motivational speeches at company events or write about them in their press releases. But these words are empty truisms quickly vanquished by the latest daily report. There's no system backing up their words so good intentions die under dollars.

"The 'rank and file' know better. What the executives say and what they do are out of integrity. Over the generations, workers have figured out they're better off to ignore the internal messaging and public relations. The executives really only care about meeting the numbers and earning their bonuses. The employees aren't skeptics; they're realists. In this regard, it's the executives who are the self-deceived idealists disengaged from the reality within the business."

Wringing my hands in nervous concern I told Bob, "I get it. We're hypocrites with 'corporate speak' straight out of a

Dilbert cartoon. Trust is undermined."

Bob nodded, "Exactly. The employer and employee are confounded by one another. The executives are casting intentions and possibilities while the employees assess past behavior and seek proof of present and future improvement. Discord, instead of unity, is sown which results in 'sides'— basically, a management side and a labor side. The division is so steeped in our early 21st-century business culture that neither side recognizes its part in the dance of this divide or its role in the repair.

"Actively disengaged employees have unfortunately adapted to their role by proudly owning their powerlessness by way of sabotage. Like crabs in a bucket, they restrain their peers from escaping this collective captivity. They breed mediocrity and offer such self-defeating statements like, 'Misery loves company. A person needs to know their place. Material success is all ill-gotten gain. Rich people are all thieves on the back of the poor. Aspirations are for the rich and my lot in life is cast. It's not what you know, it's who you know.' Such words of animosity reinforce the divide."

Bob continued, "Each side is recalcitrant and points a finger at the other side and says, 'Change!' When the real problem isn't the people but the obsolete CEO-led system, they've failed to identify as the root cause of their dissension and mutual destruction."

Struck by Bob's words I observed, "That's the opposite of 'Everyone Profits.' It's another stupid contest with both sides winning?"

Bob laughed as I continued. "This management–labor divide is ludicrous. The two sides are obviously and unnecessarily at odds when in fact they're on the same team. May I assume the CLO Integrity Map helps CLOs with resolving the standoff?"

"Definitely. Whereas an organizational chart presents and preserves hierarchy and authority, the CLO Integrity Map overlays a unifying purpose, approach, and objectives. By attracting and engaging like-motivated team members who are on-purpose when serving the customer, the notions of 'sides' and 'superiors' are displaced by mutual aspiration of serving the common good. Most people really want to know that their lives matter and can make a difference. They want their heart to be in their work—not get crushed by it. What a waste of talent!

"The CLO Integrity Map prepares and anticipates people rising to their potential once given half a chance to make their unique contribution."

Drawing an analogy to the folk tale of *The Goose That Laid The Golden Egg*, I said, "In the current CEO state, the two sides are sufficiently astute not to outright kill the goose (the business) that lays the golden egg (provides paychecks and dividends). But each side is slowly starving it, keeping the goose just short of death and minimally producing golden eggs. Each has accepted discomfort in their respective comfort zones."

Bob said, "True, but let's not beat up our CEO colleagues or their teams too much. Typically, they're all caring and decent people who want what's best for their families, team, business, and customers. For generations, however, they've gradually disintegrated into their respective roles. Neither side was aware of and therefore not equipped to profitably leverage the Articulation and Synthesis stages. It's hard to place value on the unknown.

"In contrast, the Development and Performance stages are tried and true. In this mode, both sides know how to play the game to achieve acceptable results. Inadvertently, both 'sides' are depressing their shared opportunities."

Pointing to a quote by Albert Einstein on his wall, Bob asked me to read it aloud. "We cannot solve our problems with the same thinking we used when we created them." Looking back at Bob I said, "That about sums it up the CEO dilemma."

Nodding his agreement, Bob resumed, "The CLO Integrity Map completes our toolbox and improves our opportunities to gain engagement. Many former CEOs embrace and adopt the Map to transition into our new role as CLOs. Given the choice, few of us want to just sprinkle organizational 'fix-it' fairy dust on surface symptoms that are masking the inherent flaws of the archaic CEO-system. We long for real growth and meaningful contribution. This is the way!"

Nala tops off everyone's coffee mugs. Drawing a long sip, the CLO says, "Hmmm, this *is good* coffee." Following his lead, Chris and you each take a drink and agree on the coffee —and more.

The CLO reflects, "As I recall that conversation with Bob, his insights and perspective convicted me but also inspired me with hope. As a CEO, I knew I was capable of doing a much better job of leading the business; but previously I was at a loss as to how.

"Back then, I worked earnestly on behalf of the business and team but we were caught in the dominant pattern of business feudalism.

"Bob's generous contrast of CEOs and CLOs helped me appreciate why the CLO Integrity Map is more than just words, lines, and boxes on a single piece of paper. He thrust this collective CEO blind spot before me so I could see into the blackness and choose differently. Most importantly, Bob, Hal Trudy, and my Pops were guiding me out of the darkness into the light.

"Naiveté is not an excuse, but it is too often used as one. My innocence became my positive energizer to improve as a leader, to better grasp the implications and ways of being a Chief Leadership Officer.

"Bob advised me that there's a lot more to the CLO Integrity Map than initially meets the eye. How right he was. Having whet my appetite I was ready to dive more deeply into details of the CLO Integrity Map. Bob willingly obliged by pointing to the Articulation column where he began explaining it."

Chapter 13
The On-Purpose Statements
(The Deep Strategy)

If you want to build a tall building,
start by digging a deep hole.

John Smith
Founder
College of Executives Online

CLO

Bob began, "In the Articulation column is a box holding 'Purpose, Vision, Missions, and Values,' which are collectively known as the On-Purpose Statements. They are the *deep strategy* of an organization. CLOs standardize these terms to create constancy in the language of leadership, unity in strategy, and simplicity in communications within the company culture.

"This simple practice brands the business intentions and informs the business design so the team is meaningfully connected to the purpose of the organization. Because of their personal experience with purpose, vision, missions, and values they better grasp the company's deep strategy."

Jumping in I said, "Defining terms. Wow, not doing that is the root cause for many of our problems. Looking at the left to right movement of the CLO Integrity Map, I see that confusion at the deep strategy muddles the rest of the Map. It is like addressing a golf ball on the tee and being misaligned to the target. When the initial trajectory is lined up off target even the best compensating techniques are less effective than just getting set up properly from the start."

"Yes," agreed Bob. "Integrity is impossible until we share common terms and standards. Purpose precedes integrity. It informs the structural integrity of our business model via strategy, systems, and structure. Purpose also provides leadership integrity in and between the intrapersonal and interpersonal levels.

"The first articulation of those standards is the articulation of a unique organizational purpose. Linking the company to the shared business purpose of Increasing Wealth is finding bedrock.

"Such anchoring lays a business foundation and cornerstone for the rest of the business design and build. The purpose of the organization, therefore, is the ultimate touchpoint for aligning and integrating the entirety of the CLO Integrity Map.

"There's a wonderful payoff going from a CEO to a CLO. As a CLO the weight of my leadership responsibility is getting it right in the Articulation and Synthesis stages and guiding organizational alignment and integration. Thanks to the Map, my job is ten times more effective because the team uses common language and processes.

"I used to be negligent on this facet of organizational leadership. Once every year or so I would call for an executive retreat where we might write or revise our business strategy and focus. We would debate our mission or vision, but we didn't have an agreed upon standard definition or understanding. Our language of leadership and strategy was confused so we were confused, but that didn't stop us from proceeding with making strategic plans. Disconnection from the deep strategy was almost immediate because we anxiously moved to money-making and money-tracking activities.

"As a CEO my underlying assumption was that strategy is an executive function—not a concern of the rest of the team. Their job was to execute on the strategy we devised ... or so I thought.

"Keeping team members out of the strategic loop is an erroneous assumption. It is, however, an effective means for preserving power and control. Team members are constantly turning to the executive in charge for answers. Of course, more independently minded managers will fill in the strategic and leadership vacuum with their interpretation of company initiatives.

"Thanks to my c-suite peers and my bottleneck decisions, we slowed down the business fluidity. Such unhealthy codependence births chaos and bureaucracy."

The Folly of Being Indispensable

"Because my days were filled with attending meetings, reviewing reports, making decisions, and solving team members' problems, I actually thought I was leading. By mistakenly equating decision-making as leadership I pinched this capacity from my team members."

"I give up." I asked Bob, "So you mentioned this 'wonderful payoff.' I'm still waiting to hear it."

Bob laughed and said, "Discovering that I was dispensable made me more effective, efficient, and engaging."

I countered, "You mean being indispensable?"

Again Bob laughed, "No, I said *dispensable*.

"When I thought I was indispensable, the business revolved around me. Such ego stroking left me with feelings of superiority. I convinced myself I was being a 'good servant-leader.' Bizarrely I moaned about my team's lack of stepping up in order to create a self-justifying evening drive home regaling in my amazing wonderfulness. *What would they do without me?* Drunk on ego and power, my thinking was so clouded that I was blinded by the overwhelming evidence that my lack of leading was the source of far too many situations that needed me to step in to fix them. I was indispensable because I thrived on the chaos I created. Thanks to the feudalism of the CEO-centric command and control business operating system, I was surrounded by loyal subjects, not teammates who could safely approach and confront me for the good of the company.

"This was my little professional purgatory. Instead of equipping my team to succeed without me, the net effect of my indispensable management style was conscription into dependency. I was an emperor, not a leader. Talented people with options left the business for more engaging opportunities. Who wants to work for a self-indulgent, controlling ruler leaning dangerously close to being a profit-taking tyrant?

"Rather than working to replace and free myself for more growth, my self-importance fed on being as necessary to as many people as possible. I had become an arrogant jerk surrounded by people willing to tolerate it. The net effect was the remaining team members were either very loyal or without options, 'yes men,' or disengaged paycheck pullers. With little exception I was lording over a weak team at best."

Bob confided, "I have few regrets in my life. But I do wish I had embraced my dispensability sooner. When the lights came on for me I changed my ways fast. Everything changed for the better once I parked my petty ego to the side and focused on leading the business instead of running it."

Moments of Leadership Development

"What did you do differently?" I asked Bob.

He responded, "I followed the Map."

I reminded him, "Previously you mentioned leadership training where you invested in the team writing personal on-purpose statements and applying the Map to their careers. Is that where you saw payback on your investment?"

"Yes. That strengthened team members and sent a message about the transformation of our culture to being a company of leaders. As the team's leadership quotient improved and I stopped meddling, team members lead in the jobs they were hired to do in accord with the company purpose and plan.

"Thanks to the Map, our planning and communications steadily improved. We gradually transformed into more of a self-organizing, adaptable team of leaders. Blessedly I was no longer so indispensable. In fact, I was surrounded by strategic team members who were far better informed and equipped to make local decisions. They might consult me, but I left their decisions with them."

"But you still make decisions, right?"

"Absolutely, but the decisions I make rise to the scale and scope of my office and accountability."

"Which is?"

"Generally, matters related to the three charges of a CLO. Specifically, oversight of the CLO Integrity Map and our three bottom lines. I'm the keeper of the company purpose and the ultimate integrator of the business."

Bob placed the tip of his pen on the On-Purpose Pal. "This happy little guy translates the technical talk of deep strategy into an imagery that's more viscerally understood and memorable to our team members. He makes deep strategy more usable in everyday conversations, situations, and decisions. Through him, even elementary school–aged kids can learn deep strategy. Such simplicity provides team members with clear guidelines that spurs greater confidence and independence. There's a learning curve, but once this leadership approach is in play, it's hard to imagine going back to the old command and control style."

Easing his pen point along the CLO Integrity Map, Bob said, "The On-Purpose Pal 'tells' the Strategic Story. This unifies us and communicates why our work matters. Stakeholders pick it up and pass it along word-of-mouth."

I noted, "So the Synthesis stage creates a more user-friendly understanding and application of the deep strategy."

"Well said," agreed Bob.

Bob continued, "I used to see people as 'human resources,' and I hate to admit this: at times they were faceless units of production—pieces on my business board game. These 'assets' served at my command and were to do what they were told or there would be hell to pay. As their 'superior' I needed them to do their job, period.

Shared Variance

"Every variance from the norm was an annoyance. The employee was always the first person to be blamed because they were at the spot of the problem. As management, we stepped in to bring them in line or to fire them and hire someone else who would do the job right.

"Today, problems are guideposts to improvement, not episodes to be feared. When there's a problem, we first assume it is a shared variance—a breakdown in the system not the person. Reviewing the Map we search for system flaws or training deficits that might have contributed to the problem arising. This collaborative approach avoids costly ass-covering and more rapidly leads to retooling that minimizes repeating a mistake."

I reflected with Bob, "Collaborating sounds like a more civil way of solving problems."

Bob laughed, "No more circular firing squads surrounding the 'problem' team member."

I jokingly surmised, "So everyone's not all over the map, huh?"

Bob chuckled, "Actually we *are* all-1-1 over the Map in terms of improvement. Disarray, as you are implying, that's a rarity anymore."

"This sounds great. Let me ask, a lot of companies focus on employee retention programs to keep their best and brightest people. How do CLOs address this?"

Bob made a face. "Ugh, the language of CEOs is so subtly disheartening and distancing. A phrase like 'best and brightest' waxes poetic, but what does it say about the rest of the 'bumpkins' on the team? 'You're not so good and not so bright.'

"We don't need a retention program. The Map naturally engages people in meaningful and significant work. Either a person is a mutual fit or not. If not, then we don't hire them or we amicably part ways. It's that basic.

"Leaders release the highest and best use of each person's purpose, visions, talent, and strengths for the highest and best use on the team."

A skeptical Chris says, "I don't know. Looks good in theory, but does this CLO stuff and the Map work in practice?"

The CLO says, "Before the Map, our efforts were sincere but disjointed and ad hoc—all over the map as I had joked with Bob. We were constantly in a reactive 'patch-it-up' mode. I was the only person integrating anything—an exhausted me, I should add. The On-Purpose Statements connected the team at the deepest levels so across the entire Map we were teammates not competitors. Common process frees remarkable previously untapped talent and brain power to focus on what matters the most.

"Within their area of responsibility, team members systematically improve our 'operating system,' not just fix an endless series of problems. They're self-motivated because they understand the importance of their role in context and they see their contribution to the whole extending through our Customer Chain and beyond to all stakeholders. Such preparation, contact, and follow-through works.

"The power of common language and common process aligned to a common purpose is a beautiful way to do business."

Ever the jokester, Chris says, "So this Map, it's the elusive Bigfoot of Business?"

This comment stumps the CLO. Sometimes Chris's wit

and references are just too obtuse. Looking at you for guidance and getting none, a shrug of your shoulders told him you didn't have a clue what Chris is referring to.

Chris says, "Come on guys. How many times have you said or heard, 'We need to get everyone on the same page'? This Map, this is it! This is how we get it done! Bigfoot exists."

"Chris, you're a piece of work," says the CLO. "In a thousand years, I would never relate the CLO Integrity Map to Bigfoot. Why not? Yes, this is the Bigfoot of Business—the means to develop a more cohesive team and get people on the same page. Instead of forcing conformity, we gather around mutual self-interest as stated by our On-Purpose Statements."

Self-satisfied with his folklore contribution to the CLO body of work, Chris presses on, "Let me clarify. Earlier you said the Map helps you to fulfill your charges as a CLO to position both the company and the people to be leaders and then integrate them. The Integrity Map lays out the pathway for doing that. Right?"

"Indeed," emphasizes the CLO.

Money, Management, and Meaning

Chris begins summarizing aloud to ensure he understood the CLO, "As a CEO I use two primary levers or tools to control my business: money and management. Money is controlled through a budget. Management is controlled through an organizational chart and business plan. In these documents I define and delineate people, roles, and responsibilities. These are the primary devices CEOs use to run their companies. Right?"

Nodding his head in agreement, the CLO and you continue listening to Chris, "Money and management, however, are incomplete. For all the good they do, they highly favor the tangible over the intangible. The inherent value of people and the profound meaning of work are all but neglected. Purpose adds the benefits of a third dimension: Meaning. Guys, am I still on track?"

"Yes," confirms the CLO.

Chris is on a roll, "Elevating meaning to its rightful place to be on par with money and management seems like it's adding a third dimension: leading. The interplay of money, management, and meaning is a more complete basis for business leaders.

"Every person searches for meaning. Yet businesses don't really address that need. What an oversight! How could we be so blind?"

Turning to the CLO Chris says, "Let's get back to the Bigfoot of Business. What are some other ways you help business owners like me get everyone meaningfully on the same page?"

Chapter 14
The On-Purpose Pal

The line it is drawn the curse it is cast
The slow one now will later be fast
As the present now will later be past
The order is rapidly fadin'
And the first one now will later be last
For the times they are a' changin'!

The Times They Are A-Changin'
Bob Dylan
Singer-songwriter and 2016 Nobel Laureate

Bob said, "The On-Purpose Pal makes the On-Purpose Statements more user-friendly. Let's invite him into the conversation now."

I clarified, "The cartoon character between Articulation and Synthesis?"

Bob smiled as if seeing an old friend. "Yes. That little guy is the On-Purpose Pal. Let me introduce you.

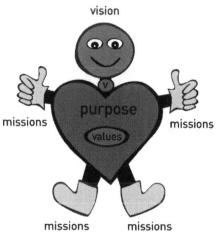

"Standing and smiling confidently between Articulation and Synthesis he makes the Strategic Story content box into a speech bubble. His visual presence on the Map gives both voice and visceral references to purpose, vision, missions, and values.

"The On-Purpose Pal is every CLO's friend for communicating and training stakeholders—the board, c-suite, team members, customers, vendors, and the public. As a likable and modest cartoon character, he conveys sophisticated leadership and strategy concepts to the point where even young children can understand and apply them."

"Purpose, vision, missions, and values are used in everyday conversation, so people have a light understanding of them. This carries over into the leadership and strategy conversation where these vital terms are loosely interchanged and ill-defined. The lack of a shared convention makes for confused people, tactical misinterpretation, incomplete actions, and haphazard performance throughout the remaining stages of the CLO Integrity Map. Fortunately, the On-Purpose Pal depicts the standard language of leadership and strategy while making each term easier to relate to and comprehend.

"Words are powerful and creative. They bring ideas and actions to life. These specific words—purpose, vision, missions, and values—are the language of leadership and strategy. Therefore, we CLOs have a duty to be crystal clear on their meaning as well as the unique articulation of each word in our organizations."

"Within the On-Purpose Statements, each word has a precise stand-alone meaning as well as a mutually supportive relationship to the others. As to the order, we always write or speak of them in this specific sequence: purpose, vision, missions, and values. Looking at the On-Purpose Pal this means we start with the heart (purpose), go to the head (vision), then the hands and feet (missions); and all of this is governed by our throat and gut (values). The heart is a powerful metaphor on many levels, including representing purpose. It is the source, the beginning point of strategy which sparks a vision that is brought to life through missions and is guided by values."

"Bob," I admitted, "I've never given any thought to the

'language of leadership and strategy.' I'm a tech guy running a business. My strategy was simple: make enough money to meet payroll, then pay the bills, and finally cut a check for me."

Bob empathized, "Once I was no different. Survival and strategy didn't seem to mix. Most entrepreneurs start that way and remain in survival mode because there's never a good time to work on the business strategy.

"Of course my business had the perfunctory, generic sounding mission statement, but it was just that. It described what the business does, not who we were, why our work matters, or what was important to our way of doing business.

"The CLO approach helped me realize that strategy is the only way out of survival mode. Before, I was caught in what I call 'Hellegation,' the place where business leaders get stuck and from where they can't seem to escape.

"The On-Purpose Pal demystifies strategy and provides an easy 'full-bodied' visual for the relevance and relationship to our business operations. He helped me finish this unfinished business. My clarity carried into the team. We were much more of one mind. It was almost too easy.

"Traditionally, the deep strategic conversation is confined to high-level corporate meetings. The Board, CEO, and c-suite officers are legally the seats of corporate authority, policies, and ends. They tend, however, to act like Moses did with God. They go away to a mountain top. Some time later they return with a set of commandments to direct and judge the people. Jethro, Moses' father-in-law, chided him about learning to delegate."

"Really? I never considered Moses with a father-in-law."

Bob suggested, "Ask your Pops about it sometime. The story is in his Good Book, Exodus, chapter 18. Who knows, perhaps Jethro was Taylor's original inspiration for division of labor?" We chuckled.

Bob returned to the On-Purpose Pal. "This little guy helps

me fulfill my CLO charge to position people to be leaders of their lives and work. He's vital to setting the standard for our personal and organizational purpose statements plus the respective visions, missions, and values. How else can we be a company of leaders without common language?

"When each person knows why they're here, where they want to go, how they want to get there, and what's important along the way (that's purpose, vision, missions, and values), then they've gained a personal leadership advantage. Once known, invariably a person is positioned to be a more active leader of their life. And because developing as a leader is encouraged, supported, and accepted as a company norm, team members rise into their greater leadership potential. That doesn't happen unless I, as the CLO, value people as people and am willing to invest in increasing the wealth of each person. It starts by helping them be an on-purpose person."

Bob delighted in saying, "And it gets even better. All of our personal experience with the language of leadership and strategy prepares each person to understand the company's On-Purpose Statements. Working through a person's self-interest, they are concurrently learning to be a strategic leader in, on, and with their position at work and in the company at large. Everyone profits."

The implication of what Bob shared was ingenious— offering a self-interested personal leadership development program also introduces the language of leadership and strategy across the company. The by-product of this personal insight is that it creates a common organizational language of leadership, strategy, and experience. When the team members read or hear the company's On-Purpose Statements they'll more readily grasp them. This training creates a solid foundation for building a company of leaders.

Deep Meaning Within Deep Strategy
Bob said, "The On-Purpose Pal offers even more insight

about purpose, vision, missions, and values. There are four CLO precepts our Pal conveys.

"First, each part of him symbolizes one of the On-Purpose Statement terms to make them memorable, relatable, and visceral. The heart represents purpose. The head portrays vision. The hands and feet show missions. The throat and gut depict values and connect all the parts.

"Second, as I've mentioned before, there's a specific order to purpose, vision, missions, and values. Purpose sparks vision which inspires missions. Values govern our decisions and actions. That's being on-purpose. Break this string of relationship anywhere and the deep strategy is weakened and the person or company is immediately at a disadvantage.

"Third, individuals and organizations synergistically benefit from articulating their respective and interrelated On-Purpose Statements. The On-Purpose Pal's capacity to clarify strategy and linkage is equally informative to an individual or an organization. Alignment of mutual purpose is known as the On-Purpose Principle. It is when the purpose of the person is aligned with the purpose of the organization. High alignment respectfully creates both individual and organizational significance and belonging or engagement.

"Finally, the jargon of leadership and strategy is made real and user-friendly throughout the company. There is no secret or insider code. Clear communication is possible because everyone is trained in and shares the same terms."

"Bob, he's powerful. I can see why the On-Purpose Pal is such a friend of the people."

"Candidly, as helpful as the Pal is," cautioned Bob, "he's also confrontational. He reveals to people and organizations the truth of their incompleteness. Such a deep stirring invigorates some people to run to clarity and improvement. Others run from their reality and go on the defensive—they shoot the messenger."

Bob's warning rang true. I felt a bittersweet conflict. On

one hand, I was excited about this discovery. On the other hand, I felt distressed and defensive for not knowing this before and letting down the team and myself. Weighing it out, however, the tremendous gain far exceeded my petty embarrassment. But that is me.

"How do you deal with this risk of rejection?"

"There are a number of ways, but they're beyond the scope of our conversation today. For now, let's just say that coaching and safety are important to the relationship."

Strategic Questions & Answers

Much was converging quickly. Bob's briefing on these four CLO precepts piqued my interest. I requested, "Clearly purpose, vision, missions, and values are related, yet distinctly different from one another. Can you clarify each a bit further?"

Bob pointed to the word "Purpose" smack dab in the middle of the character's chest. "Purpose is a matter of one's heart. It answers the 'why' question—'Why do we (as a company) exist?' Or, 'Why do I (as an individual) exist?' Our generic answer to the why question begins with, 'We (or I) exist to serve by …' and then there's a 2-word purpose statement."

"A 2-word purpose statement? Like Increasing Wealth?"

"Exactly. I'll get back to that in a bit," promised Bob.

Resuming his explanation, Bob said, "Vision is in the mind's eye or imagination and answers the question, 'Where are we going?' Vision is future oriented, aspirational, and inspirational, but attainable. Where purpose is permanent, many visions are achievable and are reset once accomplished. Some visions may be unending.

"Missions are represented by the hands and feet and answer the question, 'What do we do?' They're in the present and are highly measurable as in counting fingers and toes. Think of them as our day-to-day activities taking place working in the business. Missions have definite beginnings and ends. When we get distracted or unproductively busy, our missions typically suffer the consequences.

"Values are shown in two places, the throat and the gut. Values answer the question, 'What's important?' When what we value is threatened or violated we have a gagging defensive response in our throat or a gut reflex in our belly or both. We know something is wrong and our body is working to prevent us from emotionally ingesting it. Values are our deep code of conduct that keep the heart, head, hands, and feet healthier and more out of harm's way. They govern our behaviors. Some people refer to them as 'that small still voice inside of me'—that is if we'll take time to listen and to hear it.

Clarifying, "So our values are our conscience?"

Even before he spoke Bob was apologetically smiling, "What I'm about to tell you sounds like a riddle, but it isn't. Values are our conscience, but most of us are unconscious to our values. Therefore, articulating our values is a conscious effort to make the unconscious conscience conscious and, therefore, valued and even more valuable. Got that?"

Bob paused at this point to smile and give me time to sort out his statements. Replaying his 'riddle' over in my mind, it made sense. I finally said, "Got it."

Chris concedes. "I thought your flashy new 'Chief Leadership Officer' title was a cutesy corporate fashion statement. In truth, there's more here than meets the eye. This CLO thing is way more developed than I imagined."

The CLO comments, "Good. Thanks for staying open minded to this more complete leadership approach to life and work."

Chris is curious, "If I'm grasping this correctly, you're

saying that there's two potential strategic missteps: ill-defined strategic terms and incomplete strategy. The On-Purpose Pal anchors the terms for purpose, vision, missions, and values. Therefore, ill-defined terms are no longer an issue. And if we articulate all of the On-Purpose Statements, then our strategy is built on solid ground and complete in concept? Of course planning and execution follow—building out the Map."

"True," says the CLO.

Chris, whose voice tended to carry anyway, loudly proclaims, "I want this full-bodied approach."

Nala approaches the table and asks, "Did you say you want to try one of our more full-bodied roasts?"

Chris chuckles and politely says, "No, no, no," as he waved her off but explains. "I'm sorry. We're talking about 'full-bodied' business strategy, design, and leadership. For example, your husband and you have a full-bodied business here."

She smiles and innocently adds, "Pardon me. I don't know what that is. We just followed our hearts and the rest of the business naturally followed."

She unknowingly confirms Chris's observation and reinforced that deep strategy starts in the heart.

"While I'm here, does anyone need a refresh?" she asks.

"Yes, thank you," says the CLO. Chris and you also accept her kind offer.

Looking at his watch the CLO says, "Let's keep track of the time; I've a plane for Pittsburgh to catch. We're still good on time. Next on the CLO Integrity Map is the Strategic Story, the Synthesis stage."

Chapter 15
The Strategic Story

Clients say, "What's your strategy," and
I say, "Ask me what I believe first."
That's a far more enduring answer.

Ginni Rometty
President and CEO of IBM

CLO

Bob informed, "Leaders deal with strategy and execution, but not everyone's job is to define, develop, and deal with the core corporate strategy. Everyone in the company, however, delivers on it. Therefore, CLOs invest heavily in the Articulation and Synthesis stages to make the deep strategy appropriately known and owned by all team members.

"The On-Purpose Pal smooths the technical edges of the deep strategy found in the On-Purpose Statements. The Strategic Story takes that friendliness another step further. You've heard me say, 'Facts inform, stories transform.' For this reason alone stories play a crucial part in the communication and culture of CLO-led companies.

"People relate to stories and stories relate to people. Stories convey messages and meaning that stick in people's minds better than facts and figures. Stories come in many forms and from many situations. In the business world, every business has true stories to share. There are founder's stories, customer stories, team stories, war stories, turnaround stories, and more. Strategic Stories are a special category of business narrative that reveal and reinforce aspects and elements of the deep strategy in memorable ways."

"Can you give me an example?" I asked.

Leaning back in his chair, Bob looked off to the distance thinking. He began, "In 1961, President John F. Kennedy told the US Congress, 'I believe that this nation should commit itself to achieving the goal, before this decade is out, of landing a man on the moon and returning him safely to the earth.' This was part of a larger address on 'Urgent National Needs' based on preserving freedom in response to aggression by the Soviet Union. It became an international strategic story with historic implications.

"Imagine what it was like to work at NASA then. If any person felt their work didn't matter or make a difference, they could readily return to those few simple words to draw upon the symbolism and substance of how their life and work mattered to what might otherwise seem routine. They were genuinely making history by defending the ideals of the United States of America using their brains and ballistics rather than bullets and bloodshed.

"When a cause is noble, just, and right, people instinctively rally behind it to bring it into *being*, even when the *doing* is difficult.

"Admittedly, at the R. D. Scott company, we're not putting a man on the moon, but in our own way we know that we hold a part of the promise and purpose of business to be Increasing Wealth for people on the planet. That's remarkably inspiring! Particularly when you consider any business can own this perspective if they'll just think it through."

Speaking to Bob, I said, "I recognize elements of purpose, vision, missions, and values in President Kennedy's speech. For instance, he set a *vision* with a deadline for accomplishing what seemed an impossibility at the time—putting a man on the moon. He expressed a *value* about individual life when he talked about 'returning him safely to the earth.' He focused and inspired a country to rally to a peaceful *vision* which came to life in the Apollo program space *missions*. As importantly, he sent a message to his Cuban Missile Crisis audience in the Soviet Union that the USA could and would achieve the impossible—and would win the space race. Between the lines he said, 'If we can do this in space, then don't mess with us on Earth.'"

Bob applauded me and said, "Nailed it! In fact, you took the Strategic Story and instinctively reverse engineered to the On-Purpose Statements. Plus you worked it through the CLO Integrity Map to the internal and external audiences and tied it together as an On-Purpose Customer Experience that in this case landed on July 20, 1969, and safely returned home four days later. Nicely done."

Wrapping his hands around his coffee mug, the CLO shares, "CEOs traditionally work from a belief that people are on a need-to-know basis regarding business strategy. The thinking being that employees just need to do their jobs and the strategy will fall into place.

"CLOs dispel this old school thinking. Thanks to the Digital Age, information is readily and rapidly available anyway. People are accustomed to being better informed and knowing where their work fits in.

"As a CLO I actively want team members to know who we are, why we're here, where we're going, how we're getting there, and what's important to us—our identity as defined by our purpose, vision, missions, and values, respectively. Answers to these questions set an open tone and solid foundation for trust and engagement. This stimulates strategic unity and integration—which in turn offers valuable intangible competitive advantages. A shared identity and purpose binds us as a team and is a superior intrinsic motivator compared to the carrot and stick, extrinsic management methods leftover from the thinking of the Industrial Age."

Moving his wooden coffee stirrer along the CLO Integrity Map, the CLO says, "The Strategic Story informs the Development and Performance stages. Strategic advantages create fluidity through brand improvement, lower costs, attracting and retaining top performers, smoother working relationships, and more."

Chris observes, "So the Articulation and Synthesis stages are a conduit to flow the energy of purpose the length of the Map? They fill the space between deep strategy and frontline execution?"

"Exactly, Chris," answers the CLO. "Synthesis is the act of turning the purpose, vision, missions, and values into a Strategic Story so it can inform the Business Strategy and Communications Plan branches which rejoin to create the complete customer experience."

"I've a nuts and bolts question for you," says Chris. "Bob gave you an example of writing a Strategic Story, but how do I go about writing one for my company?"

"It's there! Chances are you've never stepped back before and looked for it," answers the CLO. "Start listening to your company lore. Pay attention to what you tell customers or even family about your company. Also interview people to tell you about your company. Hear what team members say, especially your sales persons. Review your marketing materials and website. Write your On-Purpose Statements. The Strategic Story will emerge because bits and pieces of your Strategic Story are typically already being told.

"Your Strategic Story needs to be factual and strategically representative, but not necessarily literal. A reasonable amount of creative license or storytelling may be necessary to enliven the illustrative intent or embellish it for dramatic effect. But don't fictionalize it.

"Be audience-centric and not self-centric. The Strategic

Story is about your company, maybe even you as the founder, but tell it in the self-interest of the audience. For example, many Strategic Stories fall into the 'There must be a better way to ...' category where a bad personal experience becomes a crusade to improve something so others don't have to suffer your bad experience.

"The audience needs to see themselves in the story. You want them to relate by thinking, '*I know that feeling,*' '*I've thought about that,*' '*Yes, I've had that experience,*' or '*I know someone who has ...*'

"Whew-w," Chris breathes out. "This is a tall order."

"Take it one step at a time. Hire a copywriter who is talented at listening and reaching an audience through stories."

"How long is a typical Strategic Story?" asks Chris.

The CLO says, "They vary in length but even if you've written a book or shot a video of it, have a succinct, under a minute version. You want it to be memorable and easily retold."

"For example?"

"Susan, my insurance broker, founded and leads a local but large independent insurance agency. Her Strategic Story goes like this: Susan's father died in an automobile accident when she was nine years old. Fortunately, he owned sufficient life insurance coverage so her mother and siblings' lifestyle remained intact. She knows firsthand the benefits of having life insurance coverage.

"Pretty simple, right?" asks the CLO.

Chris and you nod in agreement.

"Based on that story alone, what attributes do you ascribe to Susan?"

Chris begins, "Committed, successful, honest, caring, digs deep to serve the client, informed, professional."

"You're right—that's Susan. But, why did you attribute those positive qualities to her?"

"Her personal experience," responds Chris, "lends itself to

assume that's the case. Her heart's in it. She turned her lemons into lemonade."

"Except," says the CLO, "Susan never shared her past with clients. She felt it was too private and didn't want to impose her life's tragedy onto others or risk using 'scare tactics.'

"When I interviewed and invited her to go from being a CEO to a CLO, that's when this fact of her life came out. It fueled her passion for her industry but she kept it to herself.

"Since, her previously privately curated Strategic Story is transforming her life and those around her and beyond. She used to be a moderately successful insurance sales person. From the time she started sharing this defining moment in her life, her business took off. Her Strategic Story gave her permission to stop selling insurance and to be more fully present and personally concerned about the well-being of her clients. They know Susan cares, period.

"Her insurance expertise was unchanged, but her authenticity and leadership emerged. Like you, her prospects and clients intuitively linked why she was in her business and why they are more than a case number to her. Because of her tragedy, they believed she would do right by them, and they were right. Because her story is simple and compelling, her clients and colleagues easily remember and retell her story just as I did to you. As her story traveled, her reputation grew and so did her clientele."

"Amazing!" marvels Chris.

The CLO says, "It gets better. Following the CLO Integrity Map, Susan began searching for possible team members with what she calls, 'stories with appreciable firsthand insurance benefit.' Such experiences might include the premature loss of a parent, a house fire, major medical or disability issues, long term care, or similar life events where insurance proceeds made a positive difference in the life of the person or their family. People even referred agents looking for a new agency to her. Now there's an entire company of agents and staff with causes and motivations that are similar to Susan's.

"In Susan's agency empathy, not surprisingly, is a company value."

Chris smiles, "Wow, it all fits together so naturally. There's nothing contrived or manufactured for the sake of marketing is there?"

"Truth," says the CLO, "always prevails. When we stand on the side of truth we're in integrity. And when we don't ... well, you know how that goes, the truth will eventually come out against us instead of working for us."

Insuring the Future

"Eventually Susan wrote up a longer version of her Strategic Story as an inspirational, life lessons book about her experience growing up without a father. She shares with living fathers what they can do to prepare their children for life with or without them. She offers insights and suggestions of fun activities and meaningful moments her brothers and she missed being without a dad. She's also written a children's book for kids who have had a parent unexpectedly die or become incapacitated.

"Book sales fund her community service work with families who prematurely lost a parent, many of whom are veterans. Everyone profits with this book because a not-for-profit agency gets funding, fathers become better dads, children are cared for, and, guess what happens to Susan's business?"

"Her phone rings with referrals because everyone knows Susan," sighs Chris with a feigned measure of envy. "She seems to personifies increasing wealth so everyone profits Strategic Story."

"Exactly! The CLO Integrity Map isn't a technique to be manipulated by phonies. Susan's Strategic Story works because it is grounded in truth and sincerity. Susan has organically and creatively integrated her story into the Development and Performance stages on the Map.

"Stories have always been powerful communicators. A Strategic Story relative to a person and an organization is a very specific type of story because of the personal and organizational implications. Seeing the connection between deep strategy and story as helped by the On-Purpose Pal makes all the technical aspects of strategy far more tactically useful across the team."

Chris adds, "True to its name, the CLO Integrity Map creates genuine integrity far beyond one insurance sales person and her team."

"Not quite, Chris," says the CLO. "The Map doesn't *create* integrity. It amplifies existing integrity so it is transferable from one person to many."

Letting out a small gasp of recognition, Chris says, "Whoa, this is deeper strategy than I imagined. What if I'm a, and I'm not saying I am, and if you say I am I'll deny I ever said it; but what if I'm just not that deep of a person?"

"Oh my God, Chris, you are a hoot," laughs the CLO. "Yes, this is a deep message in a shallow world, but that doesn't mean you lack depth. Every person has depth because every person has a purpose. When we live from our purpose or we're being on-purpose, then we're living true to ourselves and the depth of our design.

"We all start as journeyman leaders. Allow time to mine the depths of your being and to discover your purpose. The crucible of life and work will refine it and forge it into your unique leadership mettle."

"Whew," says Chris with a sigh of relief. "I was concerned there for a minute."

The CLO says, "Now, let's get back to a promise Bob made me to talk about 2-word purpose statements."

Chapter 16
The 2-Word Purpose Statement

I have made this letter longer than usual
because I lack the time to make it shorter.

Blaise Pascal
French Mathematician
1623–1662

CLO

The possibility of reducing my business to a unique 2-word purpose statement seemed too simplistic to be useful and, frankly, just plain gimmicky. Of course, I had the same impression about the On-Purpose Pal. It was intriguing.

Bob said, "The starting point for the CLO Integrity Map is the purpose of the organization. Distilling a business purpose to two words may appear daunting, but once written, its value and power courses through the Map and beyond. It becomes a reference point whereby every decision, every dollar invested, every person hired, and every tangible and intangible asset can be assessed as either off- or on-purpose. This binary clarity of being 'off- or on-purpose' liberates us to be more mindful and aligned to the deep strategy."

Anticipating the benefits, I said, "This degree of simplicity holds obvious appeal. Anything to ease my leadership load is appreciated."

Bob painted a picture, "Imagine a moment when, thanks to the On-Purpose Pal, every person on your team understands and appropriately uses purpose, vision, missions, and values. Now imagine that your business has a 2-word purpose statement anchoring its deep strategy and woven into the fabric of the company culture, operations, brand, and integrated customer experience. And, your team members know and relate to it all."

"Bob, with all due respect, you're still in the abstract. How do I write an actual 2-word purpose statement? If I've learned anything about these CLO precepts it's that they're fundamental, yet rich with layers of thought and practical implications. So, feed me something I can chew on!"

At this point, even the twinkle in Bob's eye had a twinkle in it. He obviously delighted in this question. He shared, "The 2-word purpose statement structure is simple. For an organization it starts with the generic set-up of, 'We exist to serve by ... ' and is followed by two words. For a person, it begins with, 'I exist to serve by ... ' and is followed by two words. In both cases, the first word is a gerund and the second word is an object."

"A ger-what?" I asked.

Bob spelled, "A g-e-r-u-n-d, gerund."

I shrugged, "Okay, whatever. I'm all ears."

He laughed, "Great! The first time your Pops and Hal explained it to me I thought they said 'a gerbil.' A gerund isn't a rodent. A gerund is a grammatical term. In layman's language, think of it as an action verb ending in –ing."

I asked, "For example?"

Bob said, "I can do better than that. Remember when we talked about why business exists in society?"

"Yes. We agreed that business serves people by Increasing Wealth, in terms of weal or well-being, far beyond the popular notion of financial success."

No sooner had these words left my mouth when I said, "I see. 'Increasing Wealth' is an example of a 2-word purpose statement. It answers the question, 'Why does business exist within society?'"

Bob affirmed, "Yes. Let's conjugate 'increasing.' In the past, business people were *increasing* wealth. Today, business people are *increasing* wealth. And, tomorrow, business people will be *increasing* wealth. So the gerund lends a timeless quality to the 2-word purpose statement because it includes our past, present, and future.

"I like that," I added.

"It also indicates an ongoing activity versus a finite event. Using an incorrect form, if the 2-word purpose read, 'Increase Wealth,' then as soon as a business made one penny more or one life better then it has fulfilled its purpose. Done! End of story!

"But that's absurd," Bob said. "Thanks to the gerund, 'increasing' implies there's more to come, more to learn, greater aspiration. Purpose is an enduring, permanent expression of our reason for being, not a one and done event. That's why we talk about being on-purpose beyond purpose. Being on-purpose is ongoing."

Thinking aloud with Bob, I said, "Living or doing business on-purpose must be a simpler, more direct way to be. If I'm true to my purpose, then improvement would seem to surely follow."

On-Purpose: Constancy of Purpose

"Yes. That's because purpose precedes quality. W. Edwards Deming, considered to be the father of the modern quality movement, had fourteen key principles for quality management. His first key is, 'Create constancy of purpose toward improvement of the product and service, with the aim to become competitive and to stay in business, and to provide jobs.'"

I postulated, "To some degree, he must have stood on the shoulders of Taylor in terms of productivity. It also sounds like he was attempting to humanize some of the extremes of the Industrial Age."

Bob informed, "Dr. Deming was born in 1900 and died in 1993. Just after World War II, his philosophies were widely adopted by Japanese manufacturers and had a massive influence on that country's rebuilding success. In the latter years of Deming's life, his contribution grew in prominence in the USA and around the world."

Bob said, "There's a repeating theme about purpose and leadership. Purpose is the organizational seed, the spiritual DNA, if you will, to the strategy, structure, systems, and people—the CLO Integrity Map. If purpose isn't coursing through a company, then the vision, missions, and values ring hollow which dampens performance. Contrast this thin veneer of engagement with the solid core of having a reason for being and having our heart in our work. It's a world of difference."

Considering what Bob shared, I concluded, "That means that any improvement initiative, such as a quality program or leadership training, must be grounded, as Deming espoused, in the purpose of the organization."

"Yes," acknowledged Bob. "As the ancient parable advises, build your house on solid rock instead of shifting sand for it to endure. Purpose is the bedrock for building a life or an organization. The seemingly minuscule 2-word purpose statement has gigantic impact. The entire CLO Integrity Map springs from this tiny kernel of truth."

Chris states, "Really? So no purpose, no truth; and no truth, no integrity?"

The CLO nods his agreement.

Chris presses on, "Why two words for a purpose statement? I've never heard of anything like that before."

"Why just two words?" reiterates the CLO. "The answer is simplicity, memorability, power and, importantly, it works! In the absence of deep strategy, it is easy to get sucked into shallow complexities. Here's an internal gyroscope navigating and orientating."

"Okay, then the $64,000 question is," poses Chris, "how do I write a 2-word purpose statement? This seems next to impossible. Plus since it's so important to the CLO Integrity Map, I want to get it right."

The CLO answers, "There's a temporary quick fix. Borrow Increasing Wealth as your company purpose.

"Really? I can borrow Increasing Wealth?" asks Chris. "Isn't this cheating the 'integrity' of the Map?"

"Chris, you're on a learning curve to use the entirety of the Map. Your team and you are novices. Even if you wrote a 2-word purpose statement today, you'll likely refine it in the future anyway."

"But," Chris says, "I thought they didn't change."

"They don't," offers the CLO. "With use and time often our insight in purpose improves and necessitates a rewrite.

"Think of the 2-word purpose statement as learning how to hit a serve in tennis. The stroke puts the ball in play but to actually play the game, you need to learn all of the strokes: forehand, backhand, lob, overhead, volley, and drop shot. Get on the court and start practicing and playing the game. You wouldn't wait until you had the perfect serve to start learning the other strokes. With experience, every part of your play will improve.

"Similarly, if you delay your development of the CLO Integrity Map until you have the perfect 2-word purpose statement, then you're not in the game. If necessary, borrow Increasing Wealth until your company's unique 2-word purpose statement is written, preferably sooner rather than later."

Chris asks, "Can I go to a 'tennis pro' and get it done right from the start?"

"Certainly," the CLO says. "There are professionals with the expertise to help with every stage and component the length of the Map. When you're ready I will introduce you to some CLO Pros."

Chapter 17
The Void

Marion Wade, our founder, used to remind us,
"Money is like manure.
It doesn't smell any better the more you pile it up."
If we focused exclusively on profit,
we would be a firm that had failed to nurture its soul.

C. William Pollard
The Soul of the Firm
Former CEO and Chairman Emeritus of ServiceMaster
Corporation

CLC

I observed, "Bob, it seems to me that very few companies today have a 2-word purpose statement; yet they're operating, taking care of customers, making money, employing people, and being successful in traditional business measures. So what if a company doesn't understand or have a stated purpose, let alone a 2-word purpose?"

"Let's just say there's a void in its soul," Bob informed.

I asked, "And that's a problem?"

Shrugging, Bob said, "It doesn't matter what I think. What do you think? Is there a hole in your soul?"

I confided, "In my quieter moments I sometimes wonder if there isn't more to life than just working to pay the bills. Stuff like that. I can't afford to dwell on those thoughts for too long or I'll be out of business."

Bob remarked, "That's an interesting assumption. I say you can't afford to ignore that 'stuff,' otherwise why be in business?"

I answered, "To make money for the shareholders."

"Which is an incompletely right response," said Bob.

I countered, "Now I understand now, but I thought I was supposed to just suck it up, stuff those thoughts, and get back to work."

"How's that been working?"

"I supposed that's why Pops introduced us. My work fills my 'void' with a sense of meaning and purpose."

"That last sentence isn't even incompletely right," Bob stated matter-of-factly.

This correction struck me as being uncharacteristically direct so I defended my statement, "But my work *does* give my life meaning."

"No, it doesn't," Bob stated. "You're toiling, not working. Purpose is not earned or conditional. It is. It exists. Your life has inherent meaning and purpose, period. Work is an expression of your purpose. Hopefully, one for which you are exceptionally well fitted. You bring meaning to the work, not the other way around."

"Really?"

Bob said, "Consider this: if work is your source of meaning, then your well-being and power are given over to an occupation of your time. Is that really what you want as the source of your identity and reason for being?"

"I don't think so."

Emphatically, Bob said, "Don't! Trust me, such a misplaced identity is empty and unhealthy. The vacuum in your soul must be filled with something. Your 2-word purpose puts words around it. Otherwise, you'll fill the hole with something counterfeit or a passing fancy."

"Like being a workaholic?"

"Yes, like being a workaholic."

I asked, "The Industrial Age strikes again?"

"You bet! For generations, we've been conditioned to conform to the needs of industry. Work is our identity, our provision, our status, and eventually our demise. Even the so-called 'American Dream' has undertones of being cogs in the wheels of commerce."

"Human resources," I noted.

"Yes. There's an awakening, a reformation taking place. It has to do with respecting the body, mind, and spirit of each person starting with self-care. There's an old adage, 'We're human beings, not human doings.' In other words, each of us has natural worth and rights apart from our work status.

"When each person is a better leader of his or her life and work, then everyone profits. Knowing one's purpose in life is a significant strategic and practical advantage tied to our inherent worth and rights."

As Bob painted this idealistic reality, I posed, "So if lifting people up raises us all up, I guess the opposite is true of put downs?"

"Of course," Bob confirmed.

"You sound like you want to eradicate meaninglessness?"

He replied, "Why not right the wrongs by battling the bad guys who give business a bad name by creating soulless enterprises? They trivialize life, people, and business with such sayings as, 'At the end of the day, it's just business.' They may make money, but they destroy lives in the process. They don't build relationships, trust, or a better planet. Such erroneous thinking depreciates the common wealth.

"Instead, imagine working in an enterprise where every person is actively engaged in a meaningful life being expressed through their work. They're on-purpose persons working in on-purpose businesses."

I recognized it, "That's true weal! Increasing wealth so everyone profits."

"Exactly," exclaimed Bob with a subtle down-low fist pump. "Most CEOs are not indifferent, soulless mercenaries only in it for the money. Rather, they've been reared with a distorted mindset and manner whereby business is managing scarcity rather than leading into abundance. The resulting

CEO-system has evolved to become an increasingly inhospitable host to the betterment of humanity all the while preaching service to the customer but at the expense of the employees."

Bob leaned in close to me and looked me square in the eyes, "You're not alone. The frustration you shared with your Pops is shared by start-up entrepreneurs to Fortune 100 CEOs and those in between. CLOs are the natural progression in business leadership development. Agreed?"

Shrugging my shoulders I said, "There's so much to process. As disturbing as my current situation is, the ideas and ideals of being a CLO are very disruptive."

I observed, "You're all in with being a CLO, aren't you?"

"Yes," said Bob, "Once Hal and your Pops awakened me to the obsolescence, remaining mired in the past held no appeal to me. The renewal started here," Bob pointed to his heart, "knowing I had a purpose and this business was a platform for bringing it to life helps my soul to be well.

"In the early 1950s, your Pops foresaw a needed business reformation and pioneered it in his business. Market and social conditions today are far more favorable to being a Chief Leadership Officer."

I asked, "But how?"

"Innovate! CLOs are the next generation business leadership system and model."

Chris comments, "We CEOs are inexperienced in the Articulation and Synthesis stages, yet it appears those early stages are critical to being a CLO."

"Right on both counts. Leverage your experience in the Development and Performance stages. This familiar ground on the Map makes it a far easier transition than you might be imagining."

The CLO reminds Chris, "There are reasons why we call it 'the CLO Integrity Map.' Like any map, there are more detailed versions and guides. I'll email you some later today while I'm waiting in the boarding gate area."

Integrity Matters

"That would be great," says Chris. "Why is it called the CLO *Integrity* Map?"

The CLO asks, "What does integrity mean to you?"

"Honesty, true to one's word, morally principled," Chris offers.

"You mean the opposite of you," razzes the CLO.

"Ha, ha," feigns Chris. "Stick to your shtick. Leave the trash talking to me."

Knowing better than to get into a battle of barbs with caustic Chris, the CLO heeded the advice and says, "As CLOs, we aspire to live the virtues you mentioned.

"Integrity also means to be whole, undivided, a sound state, lacking corruption, and unimpaired. The root of the word integrity is integer like a whole number versus a fraction —something fully intact versus divided.

"Integrity has word cousins such as integrate, integral, and even entirety. These are meaningful to CLOs as well. For example, purpose is integral to the Map, so CLOs integrate the business purpose along the entirety of the Map."

"But does integrity scale?"

"Yes, Chris," says the CLO. "Integrity applies to things, ideas, and more. Accompanying integrity are often standards of scale, measurement, and quality. For instance, when the standard is seaworthiness, then a rowboat and an aircraft carrier both meet the definition of integrity. If the integrity measure includes the capacity to carry jets and a crew of over one thousand souls, then the rowboat is out of integrity to the design standard."

Chris surmises, "So integrity is subject to the ship designer's intention?"

"Yes. If an organization exists to only make money, then a crime syndicate is acting within its intended design and performance standards. The Mafia is in integrity relative to that design standard. But, the mob is out of integrity with the purpose of business: Increasing Wealth (so everyone profits)."

"Wow! That's subtle, but vitally noted," replies Chris. His follow-up question is, "Much as integrity in a person implies moral upstanding, what is the basis of that morality?"

"Morality is relative to a people group. For example, two different organizations value family. One is the Mafia and the other is a family and marriage counseling center. Their respective appreciation of family is based on their peer morality and values. In the Mafia, if you cross the family, you die. In the marriage counseling center, if you cross the family you cry. Ironically both have structural integrity."

Chris asks, "But what's the controlling mechanism of morality?"

The Common Good

The CLO says, "That brings us back to purpose as the moral authority found in the soul of the person. Purpose can be thought of as each person's innate virtue or divine good."

A further cross-examining Chris asks, "So what is the 'Common Good'?"

The CLO poses, "Chris, do you want your life to make a difference?"

"Sure."

"Then that's a rudimentary version of the Common Good. Think of it as one's inborn desire to serve others. Recall the generic set-up for a 2-word purpose is, 'We (or I) exist to serve by.' Common Good is a person's free will decision to serve others. When two or more people gather together to align their respective purposes, they create a common wealth to actively pursue weal together. Sound familiar?"

"Yes, it sounds like a business with a heart and moral soul."

"Right. This 'common wealth' approach can be true of any organization. For example, in the United States of America's Declaration of Independence, Thomas Jefferson wrote that government is to protect the 'unalienable rights' of 'life, liberty and the pursuit of happiness' as 'endowed by their Creator.' Government is for and by the people so the Common Good is first and foremost the protection of those rights by and for every person.

"Robert A. Needham, JD, PhD, writing in *Collaborative Commonwealth* espouses the benefits of returning from the far extremes to a middle space known as *the Commons*. Here collaboration versus cutthroat competition allows us to transcend the inherent challenges within capitalism as we experience it. CLOs are well positioned to implement Needham's call."

"Interesting, really interesting," says Chris. "I've heard Common Good used, but never really quite appreciated it. The same with commonwealth."

Chris asks, "What about the Greater Good? Is it the same as the Common Good?"

"Bite your tongue!" The CLO informs, "They're opposites. The Greater Good is for the good of the whole or the majority of people. While that sounds democratic and noble, it places the state or collective interest above individual rights and liberties, as in Communism or Fascism. The question is this: Who decides what is the Greater Good? The moral authority is a person or group of people versus an endowment by the Creator. It presents a slippery slope. Avoid the siren song of the Greater Good."

"Can't they coexist?"

"They're incompatible. Trying to do both is crazy-making. Business leaders are confused, caught in a battle between the two belief systems, but most lack this really big picture perspective and live conflicted."

"Really?" questions Chris. "So do I need to be worried that Darth Vader is going to suddenly appear in a *Star Wars* moment and say, 'Chris, I am your father. Join me on the dark side of the Force and together we can rule the world'?"

Breaking out in a relaxed, big smile, the CLO counters, "Not if CLObi-Wan Kenobi has anything to say about it! I'm here to make you aware of the corruption of business and to be a part of winning it back to its intended purpose."

"So you're on a CLO recruiting trip?"

"In a manner of speaking. I'm sharing the CLO opportunity so you have a choice."

"About becoming a CLO, like you?" quizzes Chris.

"Yes," replies the CLO.

"Am I qualified?"

"Depends."

"On what?"

"A defining question."

"Which is?"

"Do people have a soul? Yes or no?"

Chris says, "Yes. But I haven't a clue what that has to do with running my business or why it even matters."

"That's a different matter. You've been learning about that since we sat down. Your choice, however, has profound implications in terms of how you view people and engage the fullness of the CLO Integrity Map."

"What if I said no?" asks Chris.

"Then the Map can't be energized by purpose. It is like a new car without an engine. It looks good but can't take you anywhere."

Chris says, "Now my BMW has an engine and it can take you places—like the airport. We need to leave soon. I'm flattered that you thought of me. But, really, is that all you're offering? You come to town, tell us your CLO debutant story, knock us for being CEOs, recruit us, plan on sending us an email from the boarding area, and then jump on a plane back to the Steel City. Is that all there is to this?"

"Thought you would never ask," the CLO says. "There's the CLO Foundry."

Chapter 18
The Defining Moment

Too many people think only of their own profit.
But business opportunity seldom
knocks on the door of self-centered people.
No customer ever goes to a store
merely to please the storekeeper.

Dr. Kazuo Inamori
Founder of Kyocera, DDI (now KDDI)

Bob turned to me and said, "Hal and I are inviting you to be a member of the CLO Foundry, a community of emerging CLOs. The foundry concept is a metaphor for those of us who are forging our leadership mettle as we modernize the leadership of our companies."

I asked, "The CLO Foundry? My gut response is to say, 'Yes.' Clearly, something has to change with the way I'm being in business. What's involved?"

"We meet virtually and in person. There's power in peer CLOs sharing over being in business more completely right and Increasing Wealth so everyone profits. We explore the CLO premises and principles in order to put them into practice. As peers, we share what we're learning, discuss best practices, mentor one another, and provide energy and encouragement. CLOs gathering together raises all of our standards.

"Members grant each other priority access and advice. We sustain each other through the rough patches. We're living out the Common Good in a collaborative manner."

I had no idea something like the CLO Foundry existed.

Knowing I would have access to the experiences, wisdom, and relationships with peers was comforting. I trusted Bob and Hal with acting in the best interests of the business and me. I welcomed the opportunity to become a better leader and to help the team do the same.

But I had some basic questions. "Bob, why is it called the CLO Foundry? It sounds like a mixed metaphor of the modern era and the industrial era."

Bob knowingly smiled, "The simple answer is the CLO Foundry was birthed in your Pops' conference room at the foundry decades ago. The name honors him and the CLO roots."

"Really, I had no idea."

"Since you once worked in your Pops' foundry, you know how raw materials are forged and fashioned into finished products. It seemed an apt and ironic metaphor for what we as people, not human resources, were going through to be reshaped into better leaders. Your Pops is the one who coined the expression of *Forging Our Leadership Mettle*."

"How'd the CLO Foundry come about?" I asked.

"Your Pops is like our Yoda, the *Star Wars* Jedi Master. He's a man decades ahead of his time who voiced sincere concerns about the manner in which business was being conducted in his day. But he felt powerless to make much of an impact on the business community.

"On December 31, 1972, Pittsburgh Pirates baseball legend Roberto Clemente died in an airplane crash traveling to Nicaragua as part of a humanitarian relief effort to earthquake victims. Clemente's untimely death rocked Pops and awakened him to the good that could be done for others and the preciousness of life. Clemente was only 38 years old when he died, but the most profound days of his life were not played on a baseball diamond. Pops knew it was time to go from thinking about doing business differently to acting on it.

"Soon thereafter, he confided his concerns, observations,

and methods to a then young business colleague named Hal Trudy. They began meeting regularly in the foundry conference room. In time a handful of men and women business owners got wind of what they were doing and joined them."

I noted, "So it wasn't a good old boys club?"

"Hardly. Your Pops taught us to look first at a person's character. Gender, age, race, ethnicity, or whatever were of no concern to Pops. The character of a person's soul mattered most of all.

"The early members struck upon the idea of secretly calling themselves Chief Leadership Officers instead of Chief Executive Officers. Back then, however, if they publicly went by CLO instead of CEO, no one would understand their role and responsibility.

"They called their brain trust the CLO Foundry. The metaphor stuck because it resembled the refining and shaping process of the heart, head, hands, and honor required to transition from a CEO to a CLO."

"So there are meetings? What are they like?"

"We talk business, life, and leadership. Our extended conversation today is similar to a casual meeting of the CLO Foundry. Come as my guest to a meeting and experience it for yourself."

Amazing! To me, Pops was just my great-grandfather. Through our family stories and conversations, I was well aware of Pops' business acumen and standing in the community. Listening to Bob tell it, however, I was struck by Pops' legacy. At 100, he lived a full life now free from many of the worries that consume my working contemporaries and me. I always figured his calm demeanor was just because he was really old and mellow. Now, it appeared he had been this way for many decades.

With my CEO blindspots coming to light, I dared not go it as alone any longer as I had as a CEO. I relished the thought of the stimulation and experienced guidance that Hal, Bob, and other CLOs could give to me. And I could give back to them. Had I finally found a community where I could be safe to admit my concerns, express my fears, and explore the frontiers of my leadership capacity?

And to think Pops was the point of origin for all of this. For the first time, I caught a glimpse of the reach and positive impact Pops' wonderful life was having across generations in the business community locally and beyond. And now, aside from just being his great-grandchild, I was becoming an even bigger beneficiary of his legacy.

"Whoa! Amazing!" a genuinely animated Chris exclaims. It isn't just the Ethiopian caffeine racing through his veins either. "You're carrying on your great-grandfather's vision! You're building on his legacy! You're sharing his message! That's mind-blowing!"

The CLO says, "Chris, you're missing the point. You are not alone in your CEO-to-CLO transition. Yes, the CLO Foundry is part of my Pops' legacy, and I'm in his family and business bloodline. That's my unique bonus. If I had no relationship to Pops, I would still be a CLO. I can't not share this message of Increasing Wealth and the business reformation that follows it."

Chris takes a serious note for a change, "Thanks for investing your time in us. I sincerely appreciate it," says Chris.

"I came to town to meet with several local CLOs who are starting a local chapter of the CLO Foundry, so I had to reach out to my old friend Chris. And," turning to you he says, "You're both invited.

"I'm also taking the business cards of our new colleague Nala and her husband to follow up with them. They're natural for being CLOs, plus they may be able to host some small casual gathering or even cater for the local team."

Somewhat tongue-in-cheek, Chris says, "Okay enough about you helping me; let's talk about me. The soul part of this decision seems so, well, you know, woo-woo, especially considering the impact on my woo-woo-wallet. Does this really work? What's your guy Bob have to say about that?"

Chapter 19
Souled Out

Fear is the path to the dark side ... fear leads to anger ...
anger leads to hate ... hate leads to suffering.

Yoda
The Phantom Menace
1999

CLO

The whole idea of being a CLO was too disruptive to my
psyche. Could making this unconventional title change place
my career, reputation, team, and business at risk? It was both
appealing and scary. Having worked this hard to get the
business to where it was, my hope was I could tweak a few
things here or there based on aspects of the CLO Integrity
Map.

I postured, "Bob, what you're inviting me to do feels like
heart transplant surgery for the business while it's running a
marathon. Putting the beating heart of purpose into the body
of the business and have it pulsing throughout the Map is
daunting. What's wrong with just staying a CEO?"

Bob cracked, "Nothing if you want to keep doing business
incompletely right. Being a CEO is your comfort zone. It's
known. Look, if it helps during the transition, print your
business cards to show your title as CEO-CLO."

"I can do that?"

"Sure. It's your business after all."

"That helps ease the transition."

"Good, then, that's settled," commented Bob.

"Not so fast. I'm still on the fence about all this. Does this
chief leadership officer thing work, I mean in real dollar

terms. Does it make money?"

Bob asked, "How profitable are other things in your life when they're done incompletely right?"

I laughed, "Probably not as profitable as they could be."

Bob pointed out, "An incomplete business will always produce incomplete results. Think about it: you could do business without telephones, the internet, computers, or other inventions. It would be absurd and negligent to not use these modern advantages."

"Bob, in concept, I agree with you. If I do this, how do I explain it to the board and the team—and let's not forget my wife—without sounding like I've gone off on some fad?"

Bob replied, "If you think CLO is a fad, then don't become one. You'll waffle and quit. Either it makes sense on its merits or it doesn't."

"Being a CLO makes a lot of sense."

"Then trust yourself. Build your case. Calculate your actual and opportunity costs. Assess what you have to gain. Then, speak openly and directly with your stakeholders and team about doing business more completely right as a CEO-CLO. In short, learn and lead!

"Being a CLO is the inevitable wave of the future. You can either position the business to ride it, let it pass you, or have it come crashing down on you. Why languish in the CEO past when you can prepare and prevail in the CLO future? Trust your instincts."

Looking me straight in the eyes Bob said, "This transformation from a CEO to a CLO starts with you. If you don't want to lead it, then don't do it. Please recognize that you're not even a novice CLO. It's all talk right now so you don't know what you don't know."

"Does the CLO Foundry help me with this?"

"Absolutely," responded Bob. "There's a process in place."

I confessed, "This will take some courage on my part."

Bob explained, "I understand. The root of the word

'courage' is the French word 'coeur' which translates as heart.

"When a person, such as an athlete, 'has heart,' it's a strong compliment that's referring to the person's willingness and dedication to succeed. Coaches favor this attribute for its implied strength, commitment, resilience, team play, passion, and selflessness—all the result of a love for excelling to the extent of one's abilities and team success.

Love Is The Ultimate App

"Love is symbolized by the heart, also the symbol of purpose. The heart plays a vital role in many cultures. In eastern traditions, the chakra located in the heart is the foundational spirit energy being transformed into the physical being. It means wholeness that comes from being connected to something greater than ourselves. The ancient Greeks saw the heart as a place where mind, body, and spirit were one—home to our personhood and ultimate integrity. The Jewish speak in terms of shalom, meaning peace that comes from being one with God. Christians and Jews value that 'the Lord looks at the heart' of a person to know the depth of a person. Even King David, who committed adultery and murder, begged, 'Create in me a pure heart, O God' as he wrestled to reconcile his higher intentions with his base desires and sins. In the Quran, 'a sound heart' refers to having wisdom and purity. In almost every culture, the heart symbolizes love."

I questioned Bob, "But does love have any place in business?"

With a gentle touch of sarcasm, Bob replied, "Only if you want the business integrity to be a meaningful expression of its purpose. Otherwise, feel free to occupy any old particular space for an unspecified period of time in exchange for a paycheck or salary until death do you part.

"Welcome to zombie world. Go ahead, 'live your life' looking past the present and dreaming of retirement. Prepare to die prematurely from the unhealthy habits developed over decades of failed coping with a soulless and meaningless existence. Embrace the destructive pattern of the Industrial Age employment contract. Dismiss the fact that the Digital Age is liberating opportunities for more people to actively pursue their heart's desire and you have to compete for their engagement. Avoid the coming Age of Purpose and Meaning when a seamlessly integrated life will be every person's possibility and desire. Miss out on the joyful expression of one's purpose—an authentic mark of weal. Enjoy your lower profits and harder work."

"Point taken, Bob." Dare I ask, but I did, "Bob, can a business actually have a soul?"

With his now all-too-familiar soft chuckle, Bob said, "Machines, equipment, and other inanimate objects—no. People yes. But a business can reject its soul typically in favor of making money, ergo, the human resources term and other pejoratives.

"You see love is the killer app. Any other app is counterfeit by comparison. Love is a matter of one's soul. It defies explanation. It is.

"Now does a business have a soul? It depends on what you decide about love and decide what to do about it. Does a person have the soulful capacity to love or not? Does love have a place in business? Can we love our work? Can we love another person?

"Now that you've asked about the soul of a business, it must be answered. But only you can answer it. Whichever way you choose, it will define how you see life, how you design the business and engage with other people, and what you do next. Whichever way you choose, please have the intellectual honesty to clarify and more fully integrate your selected worldview into your company. Don't be lukewarm about this decision."

Pressing him, "But Bob, do you have an opinion about a business having a soul?"

Laughing aloud this time, Bob said, "Obviously I do! I'm sold out to being souled-out. I *choose* to love my life and work. I *choose* to be as whole as possible wherever I am. If a person has a soul and a ship carries souls, then why can't a business of souls have a collective company soul?"

Chris quips, "Goodness, I feel like I'm living in the Charles Dickens' novel *A Christmas Carol*. Remember how Ebenezer Scrooge meets the Ghosts of Christmas Past, Present, and Future? Is Bob the Ghost of Christmas Past? Are you, Mr. CLO, the Ghost of Christmas Present? Are the do-good owners of Latte Out Loud the Ghosts of Christmas Future?"

The CLO informs us, "Published in 1843, during the rise of the Industrial Revolution, Dickens' cautionary tale is about the loss and ultimate redemption of one businessman's soul. Did Dickens foresee the coming ill effects being thrust on society by the Industrial Revolution? Approaching two centuries later, the moral of the story is as relevant as ever. How little has changed," he comments.

Chris frames the dilemma, "So either we have a soul or we don't, huh? I guess not choosing is defaulting to being without a soul. Either way defines me—and my business leadership approach. Right?"

The CLO says, "Yes. It is a worldview decision with subtle, yet significant implications to your core leadership approach as well as your business strategy, structure, and systems. Either you act on it or you don't. Either people are people or they're objects. You can stay a CEO or begin the journey to becoming a CLO."

The former attorney counters, "But what if the world really is so pointless as to be meaningless? What if we don't have a soul? What if there is no purpose to life or business at all? Why have ethics and ideals? Why work for the Common Good?"

Drawing in a breath, the CLO speaks, "Are you rhetorically musing aloud or are you asking?"

An emphatic Chris replies, "I'm asking."

"Then here's the straight deal, Chris. If there is no meaning, no soul, no ethic, no purpose, then you are meaningless. Our conversation today is meaningless. Your business is meaningless. What the Latte Out Loud owners are doing here and abroad is meaningless. Your friend with us is as meaningless as am I. Life is a meaningless illusion. Even your question is meaningless.

"Chris, I can't prove to you that life or business is meaningful or meaningless. I just know it is one or the other and whichever way we choose has profound implications on what we do next. And I'm calling for a verdict."

Chris presses, "But what do you believe? And why?"

The CLO speaks, "Like Bob I choose meaning. I choose to have a soul with a purpose in life. My decision has implications to how I live my life and how I am being in business. Therefore I matter in some cosmic way with my smidgen of time on the planet. And the same is true of others. We're not objects being held on the planet by gravity. We're people with bodies, minds, and spirits. I dignify this in the manner in which I conduct business.

"My choice distinguishes me from many of my CEO peers who see it differently or don't see it at all. Without prejudice, I can respect yet still disagree with their choice or lack thereof. So when I see them doing business incompletely right and I can guide them to do it more completely right, I'm compelled to approach them and engage in a conversation.

"Here's why. In a soulless existence, there is no Common Good. There's only 'My Good' or an unfettered version of what's in it for me. This egocentric, godlike posture can be harsh or benevolent, but it is still a totalitarian rule complete with subjects, not people. Unfortunately, this thinking is more prevalent in our c-suites and supervisors than we might recognize. This uncaring treatment to our 'most valuable assets' is 'justified' all in the name of making money."

"Yikes," gulps Chris.

The CLO continues, "If deep down there is no deep down, then how do managers manage, leaders lead, and sales people listen to and connect with clients? What are relationships then, really?"

"That's an interesting point," admits Chris.

"Run through the On-Purpose Pal. We've talked about the heart and love. We've talked about a worldview with a soul. Time for a gut check. On the soul side of the choice lives meaning, hope, and the Common Good. On the other side I see chaos, hopelessness, and loneliness. My gut doesn't like where that emptiness goes.

"Once I played out the implications of my options, the choice was easy for me. I chose the heroically humane path of a CLO and defied CEO convention."

Chris notes, "Years later, the evidence suggests that your business and you are thriving."

"Yes. We are," replies the CLO with a modest nod of his head. "Pounding the stake of purpose in the ground has been a positively productive and profitable business decision. I sleep better knowing that we intentionally act upon and contribute to the Common Good as a strategic end. We're not perfect but we're more complete."

Chris says, "Geez, do you realize you sound like a commercial?"

The CLO laughs as he speaks, "Chris, we've been friends for a lot of years. Show me a better way to lead and I'm all ears. As far as I can tell being a CLO works better on every conceivable level. Why not? It's the complete package.

"You ask me: Do or do not people have a soul? I did my 'soul searching' and obviously found my answer. Your gut response was 'yes,' but I see you're still pondering the implications to your business leadership. That's great. Let this fundamental life question stand free of preconceived religious beliefs or baggage you may have associated with it. It's a life question that precedes the business question. With the question now raised and for the sake of integrity, you'll need to decide if a business has a soul and what to do about it or not."

Leadership Limbo

Chris lifts his hands to shoulder level and made air quotes with his fingers as he says, "You really are 'souled' out." Recognizing Chris's artful pivoting as a dodge of the question, the CLO didn't respond.

In the midst of the pregnant pause is the crux of Chris's leadership limbo. This choice begs to be resolved. The implications aren't just about business; they're about Chris's and your respective lives.

Weighing Chris's options you calculate that taking the "no soul" route is his least disruptive path. His easy choice is to enjoy the coffee, shelve this CLO conversation, decline the invitation, and it's business as usual.

Business this way is like Darwin on Dollars—survival of the fittest finances. People are objects, relatively interchangeable pieces in the for-profit puzzle. Like emptied beer cans, once consumed they're crushed and littered on the ground.

Taking the "soul" route is awash with unknowns and a learning curve. This less traveled route holds promise to be a more profitable, whole, and meaningful destination. Building a more "completely right" business requires a renewal throughout the organization starting with the top corporate officer. It seems so risky.

When is the right time for a business disruption? It is so easy to put off. Will your team embrace the language of leadership and strategy, the CLO Integrity Map, the 2-word purpose statement, the Age of Purpose and Meaning, the Common Good, having a soul, and more? Can it work and can you lead the innovation?

On the other hand, what an amazing opportunity to renew and prepare your business and team for the future! Contemplating the possibilities for business improvement, continuity, and contribution so everyone profits is revitalizing. Tapping into the pure goodwill of the business as the coffee shop owners have done is an exhilarating possibility! But how does that translate into your business?

Lots of questions. Lots of thoughts.

Breaking his silence Chris asks the CLO, "So you truly believe that business is more than just making goods and producing services at a profit? You really see business as a platform to serve by Increasing Wealth, contributing to the Common Good, and being a place to give expression and integration to individual and organizational purpose? You believe that everyone profits is actually doable?"

"I do," says the CLO. "To be a CLO is a choice, not a requirement. But it's now your choice to make. So, let me finish my cup of coffee, then take me to the airport to catch my plane home.

"Before I leave, I'll close my strategic story of becoming a CLO and tell you what happened next with Bob ... and me."

Chapter 20
Hey, It Was More Than a Cup of Coffee

Every person has free choice.
Free to obey or disobey the Natural Laws.
Your choice determines the consequences.
Nobody ever did, or ever will,
escape the consequences of his choices.

Alfred A. Montapert
The Supreme Philosophy of Man
1970

CLO

I never did pitch Bob for his business that day. I obviously decided to become a Chief Leadership Officer and gained far more than the dollars I might have made pressing for a contract. Eventually, the R. D. Scott Company became a client through the normal channels. Bob didn't pull strings for me, nor did I ask him. Instead, our team earned the business on our merits.

The day after meeting Bob, I went to see Pops to thank him for arranging it. Pops wanted to hear all the details. As I spoke, he grinned proudly from ear to ear. This wasn't a self-satisfied grin for himself. No, his exuberance was in anticipation of what was to bear fruit in my life from a tree he planted decades before.

I continued visiting Pops regularly. He would ask me what I was learning at the CLO Foundry. He tracked the company's and my progress along the CLO Integrity Map. When I got frustrated or discouraged, he comforted me by saying, "Give it time, Great-Grandchild, give it time."

His entire life, Pops was an avid reader of business and

leadership books which he shared so we could discuss them. Even if I didn't have time to read one of his books, he would give me a book review. I jokingly called it Pops' Book Club. This was his method of keeping a watchful eye over me as a CEO-CLO, plus making sure that I was beefing up my CLO Integrity Map with fresh thinking and methods. CLO is a business operating system with a highly specific language and the Map. It is also a dynamic and alive open system friendly to diverse resources, ideas, and techniques.

The Map creates a calming effect in the otherwise stress-filled world of business. That's the power found in constancy of purpose paired with a unifying and advancing process like the Map. We're on-purpose so we're freer to focus on the content of matters and creating profitable outcomes. None of us have time for the petty trivialities of the past. With an entire team of leaders focused on results and improvement, we avoid the "flavor of the month" quick fixes.

The CLO Foundry keeps me in regular contact with Bob Scott and Hal Trudy. Bob's now close to retirement from his business and is following in Hal Trudy's footsteps to help CEOs transition into CLOs.

I eventually learned that prior to my meeting with Bob, he had never talked with another CEO about being a CLO. I was his first CLO "casting." He was as uptight as I was about the meeting, especially knowing I was Pops' great-grandchild. With all my questions, I didn't make it easy on him either. To this day, we still rib each other about it. I tell him he talked way too much, and he says I was so headstrong he had to.

I indirectly played a role in helping Bob define this next career chapter of guiding CEOs to become CLOs. That was satisfying because I felt like I was getting from him but not giving anything in return. In fact, our conversations were a classic example of "Increasing Wealth so everyone profits."

Just before Pops' 101st birthday, I sat with him talking about what he and the last year meant to many others and me.

As he advised, becoming a CLO required persevering. This experience helped me mature as a person and a leader.

Pops said to me, "Maturity is not a matter of age. Rather it is a choice. It's easy for a person to avoid adulthood and be adolescent-like even as an adult in chronological years. Sometimes maturity is thrust upon us when we or someone we love faces a life-threatening illness or accident. Death of a loved one brings reflection and perspective.

"Life choices mature us too. Marriage, for example, is an iron sharpening iron reality test. Having children brings the friction of added responsibilities which cause us to grow up. Starting a business brings a set of commitments to stakeholders that accelerates our business acumen and leadership development."

Pops also said, "Work forges and fashions you to become the person God intended you to be. Being in business tests your mettle. Let it!"

Pops was right. In fact, when I understood that "failures and challenges" were feedback and opportunities in disguise, my stress levels dropped significantly. Where there used to be crisis and panic, now I tended to be calm and clearheaded. Being a member of a team with a common language and method to co-process events and problems provided better perspectives, understanding, and decisions. Pops called that wisdom at work.

Unfortunately, Pops' advice about the death of a loved one would test my mettle too soon. The day after this conversation I got the call that Pops had awakened and eaten breakfast. He told his caregiver he was tired but wanted to sit in his chair to read his latest business book. He closed his eyes and ten minutes later when she checked on him he was dead. Ironically, he gave me one final, yet comedic opportunity to further mature. He wanted me to unceremoniously scatter his ashes at the foundry in a slag heap. Pops always told me he would be cremated because "It was a fitting way to go for a man who spent his career around furnaces and kilns." He used to joke about "being thrown in the trash heap." None of us took him seriously, however. It was what he wanted so I did it.

As he promised, I couldn't walk away from his death, but I could gain reflection and perspective on what a life of Increasing Wealth so everyone profits could be.

The CLO finishes. His eyes are a bit teary as he speaks of his Pops.

Shifting the mood in the cafe, the CLO notices the clock on the cafe wall and says, "Chris, we need to leave now for the airport."

Chris says, "Wow, you're right! As 'agreed,' I'll settle the tab with Nala."

As Chris approaches the counter to pay the bill, the CLO and you make your way to the coffee shop door. After Chris settles the check, you hold the door for Chris and the CLO to exit. Just as he's about to walk out, Chris says, "Go on out without me. I forgot something. I'll be right back and catch up with you two in a minute." He clicks his car fob to open the Beemer. The CLO opens the passenger door and puts his tablet inside the car and turns to talk with you. While the two of you chat, the CLO is gently leaning on the open car door with his back to the coffee shop.

Standing outside the coffee shop window chatting with the CLO you can look over the vehicle's roof into Latte Out Loud. You spot Chris inside and back at your table. Despite his covert attempt, Chris hasn't accounted for you spying through the coffee shop window.

Reaching into his pocket Chris yanks out his wad of cash and discreetly, but in your clear view, peels off five one hundred dollar bills one at a time. He folds them in half and then gently slides them under the CLO's coffee mug, a "tip" for Nala, her husband, and their now fully funded trip to Ethiopia. You smile.

Epilogue

Agree with each other, love each other,
be deep-spirited friends.
Don't push your way to the front;
don't sweet-talk your way to the top.
Put yourself aside, and help others get ahead.
Don't be obsessed with getting your own advantage.
Forget yourselves long enough to lend a helping hand.

Eugene H. Peterson
The Message
Paul writing to the Philippians

You run things. You make decisions. You manage a P&L. People look to you for direction and answers. You want very satisfied customers. You willingly weigh the risks and the rewards in order to make sound decisions that move the business forward.

You know the feelings of being overwhelmed and low as well as the joys and the highs of success. You persistently pursue improvement. You seek more—a better life, family, team, and customers. You strive to make a difference and make money. You willingly grasp the reigns of the beast called a business because its possibilities are endless.

Amid your inspiration, aspiration, and perspiration lives frustration. Yes, you're a Chief Executive Officer.

Now you have a fresh, heroic alternative to being a CEO. You have a choice to make about being in business more completely right and increasing wealth so everyone profits. Ask yourself, *Do I want to be a Chief Leadership Officer?*

What's Next?

CLO

1. The first step to becoming a CLO is to get connected and join the CLO movement. Stay up to date with the latest CLO thinking and opportunities.

Start by downloading the following documents:

- ✓ **The CLO Integrity Map:** A printable, color, letter-sized PDF of the Map.
- ✓ **The On-Purpose Pal:** What is the difference between purpose, vision, missions, and values? This printable, color, letter-sized PDF further clarifies the language of leadership and strategy.
- ✓ **The CLO Integrity Map Checklist:** Looking to implement the Map in your business? Use this checklist to stimulate your thinking and guide you.

To download these documents, go to:

www.CLONow.com

ONPURPOSE.me

2. The second charge of a CLO is to, "Position each person to be a leader of his or her life and work." Leadership is an inside-out development process that starts by knowing one's innate purpose. ONPURPOSE.me is an ingenious online app where, for a modest charge, you or your entire team can know their 2-word personal purpose within minutes. Corporate accounts are available by inquiring at info@on-purpose.com

www.ONPURPOSE.me

Meet Kevin W. McCarthy

Kevin is a native of Pittsburgh, PA, who lived there until 1984 when he moved to Winter Park, FL. This explains why the Steel City is a backdrop in *Chief Leadership Officer*.

Upon graduation from Shady Side Academy (SSA), Kevin attended Lehigh University and earned a BS in Business and Economics. After a year of corporate banking and then a couple more in general management of a business, Kevin attended The Darden School on the grounds of the University of Virginia. There, he earned his MBA and met Judith, his wife. (See this book's Dedication.)

Kevin's first business venture was selling candy on the school bus. As the SSA eighth-grade class president, Kevin negotiated and set up a Coca-Cola lunch room fountain concession, a first for SSA. This enterprise proved to be so profitable to the class treasury that the proceeds funded more action. For the next four years Kevin remained class president and was named "The Resident President" in his senior yearbook.

His love of the unlimited potential and creativity found in business continues. From b-school Kevin became a commercial real estate developer and President of United States Properties, Inc. After a difficult "business partner divorce," he founded US Partners, Inc., a commercial real estate advisory firm. In the late 1980s the firm transitioned to general management business consulting.

From these diverse experiences Kevin sought to improve clients' businesses and lives. This gave rise to the On-Purpose® Approach and two best selling books: *The On-Purpose Person* and *The On-Purpose Business Person*. *Chief Leadership Officer*, is the culmination of over five decades of business experiences, education, and thinking designed to elevate business leaders into the high and noble calling business is intended to be.

The On-Purpose® Books Series

On-Purpose® is a uniquely integrated approach to developing individual and organizational leadership. The set is written as easy-reading stories to engage the infrequent reader. Each book conveys foundational principles for leading a life or an organization with meaning and purpose at the heart of it. Bob Scott and Hal Trudy are characters from the set who appear in *Chief Leadership Officer*.

When *The On-Purpose Person* was originally released in 1992 by Navpress Publishing Group, there were less than a handful of people writing about purpose. This bestseller put purpose in the title and on the lips of many.

Decades later as purpose is now popularized, Kevin's pioneering work is more relevant today than when it was released. Knowing one's purpose is the relatively easy part. Living it, being on-purpose, is where the real effort and joy takes place.

The 1998 release of *The On-Purpose Business Person* addressed deep strategic challenges faced in the life and work space. This book introduced The On-Purpose Principle, The On-Purpose Pal, The Service Model, and more.

Since 2009 and 2013, both books were updated and revised to reflect Kevin's newest insights learned in the years since their original release. Learn more at:

www.on-purpose.com

Thank You Angels!

A portion of the production and marketing investment necessary to publish this book was provided by angel investors through the Publishizer.com crowd-funding platform. A sincere thank you goes out to the following organizations and individuals on this and the next page. They preordered a speech and books in good faith that *Chief Leadership Officer* would become a reality worth sharing. During my numerous rewrites of this book, the farsighted trust and commitment of these Angels uplifted me to completion.

Thank You!
Kevin

CLO Foundry Angel Investor

HIGH POINT UNIVERSITY

Dr. Nido Qubein, President

Heavenly Investors
Dr. William Lane
Robert C. McCarthy, Jr.
Dr. Ben Rall
Harry Travis

Angel Investors
(In alphabetic order by last name.)

Kristi & Thomas Alday
Lori & Dr. Wayne S.
Andersen
Cheryl & Bob Anderson
John Barret
Aldie Beard
Charles Betterton
Mark Blankespoor
Paul Brubaker
Mike Clouse
Lee Constantine
Adam Dudley
Raymond Eickhoff
Cori Freeman
Stephanie Golka
Dr. Jim Harris
Karyn & Mike Harrison
Ron Hart
Glenn D. Hettinger, AIA
Jeff Holden
Cleo Holder
June & Johan Immelman
Susan Janiak
Tami Kaiser
Robert Kennedy
Stephen Lansing

James Laverty
Richard Milam
Robin McGowan
James McLean
Susan Mogensen
Jim Morris
JoAnne Muegge
Matt Mullenweg
Diane Newman
Karen Odegard
Simon Ouderkirk
Ron Quartel
Mary Richardson
Tracie Root
Mike Samborski
Joey Santos-Jones
Jody Swain
Mary Tomlinson
Anthony Totta
John Trice
Guy Vincent
Dave Vogelpohl
Patricia Warfe
Ray Watson
David Welday
Barbara & David Zerfoss

Acknowledgments Page

The creation of a book is a lonely endeavor at the start. As the manuscript develops and moves into production it becomes a real team effort. Along this journey I pressed friends, colleagues, editors, and others into reading various versions and commenting. Each person provided meaningful feedback, sometimes without even realizing it.

Special thanks to Julie Holzmann of WordProofing.com for her diligence in copy editing and proofreading. Terry Pappy of Better3.com did a clever job of designing the CLO logo and book cover to tell the CLO story.

Thank you to the following contributors:

Adam Dudley	Dave Vogelpohl
Gordie Allen	Lee Constantine
Tana Greene	Guy Vincent
Terry Pappy	John Smith
Cheryl Anderson	Mary Tomlinson
Susan Janiak	Roger Clodfelter

Notes

Made in the USA
Columbia, SC
22 November 2017